Jerry Seinfeld

MUCH ADO ABOUT NOTHING

"Nothing in life is fun for the whole family. There are no massage parlors with ice cream and free jewelry."

Jerry Seinfeld is the master of recognition humor who packs concert halls across the country. His NBC show Seinfeld *has grown from cult status to enormous popular success. But the road hasn't always been easy; at his first stand-up performance he got up on stage and froze. This first unauthorized biography follows his rise to stardom and asks the question, Why is this man single? Also included is a behind-the-scenes look at the making of* Seinfeld, *from conception to production.*

Josh Levine has written about the arts for many magazines and newspapers. He lives in Toronto, Canada.

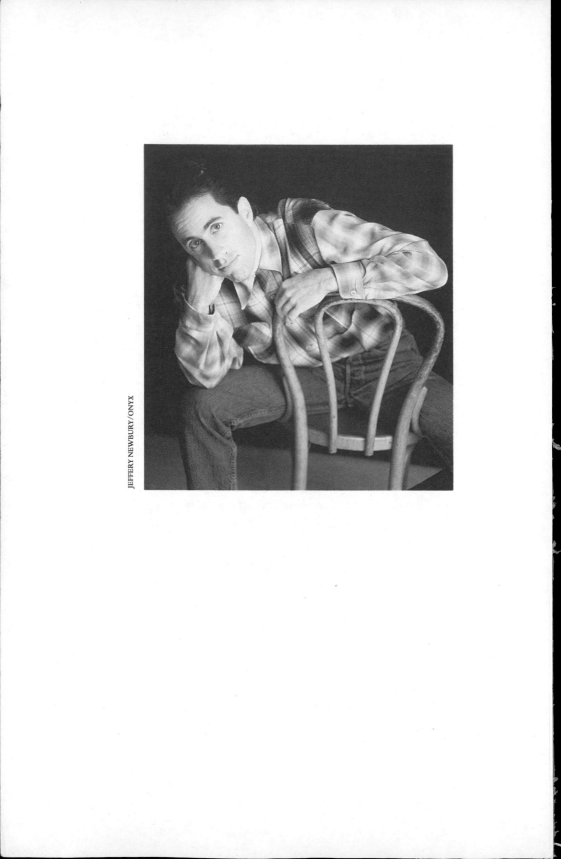

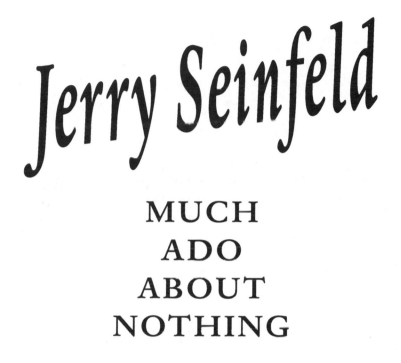

Jerry Seinfeld

MUCH
ADO
ABOUT
NOTHING

A biography by JOSH LEVINE

ECW PRESS

CANADIAN CATALOGUING IN PUBLICATION DATA

Levine, Josh
Jerry Seinfeld : much ado about nothing

ISBN 1-55022-201-5
1. Seinfeld, Jerry – Biography. 2. Comedians – United States –
Biography. 3. Television personalities – United States – Biography.
I. Title.

PN2287.S4L4 1993   792.7′028′092   C93-094912-9

COVER PHOTOGRAPHS: Darryl Estrine, Edie Baskin,
Bonnie Schiffman, Blake Little / Onyx Enterprises.

Design and imaging by ECW Type & Art, Oakville, Ontario.
Printed and bound by Imprimerie Gagné Ltée, Louiseville, Quebec.

Distributed by General Publishing Co. Limited,
30 Lesmill Road, Toronto, Ontario M3B 2T6,
(416) 445-3333, (800) 387-0172 (Canada), FAX (416) 445-5967.

Distributed to the trade in the United States exclusively by
InBook, 140 Commerce Street, P.O. Box 120261,
East Haven, Connecticut, U.S.A. 06512,
(203) 467-4257, FAX (203) 469-7697
Customer service: 1-800-253-3605 or 1-800-243-0138.

Published by ECW PRESS, 1980 Queen Street East,
Toronto, Ontario, Canada M4L 1J2

I

Tuesday Night in Milwaukee

Jerry Seinfeld's own favorite joke is the one about the detergent commercial where the perky housewife expresses delight that the product gets out bloodstains.

Seinfeld gives the audience one of *those* looks: knowing, conspiratorial, bemused, aggravated. "If you get a t-shirt with bloodstains," his voice rises with incredulity, "maybe laundry is not your problem now."

The result is an explosion of laughter from the audience and a nutshell lesson in the Seinfeld comic specialty — recognition humor. "A line like that," he told GQ magazine, "it's so solid I feel like Thor with a hammer. It's got me out of so many tight spots. Comedy is so fragile — a few good lines can save you."

Thor — who Seinfeld probably discovered in a comic book, his primary childhood reading — is one in his pantheon of superheroes. "When men are growing up and reading about Batman, Spiderman, and Superman," he once wrote, "these are not fantasies, these are options." While Seinfeld is now an adult, he still likes to imagine when he steps on stage that he is endowed with extraordinary powers. His romantic obsession with these cartoon men is part of his endearing boyish streak. Seinfeld has refused to fully grow up; he is still one of the high-school guys, ordering pizza, watching baseball, and above all cracking jokes. Even the way he views the world of a young single adult shows that he has not lost the child's peculiar perceptiveness. Friends, dating, shopping, going to the movies — he views all these subjects with the same incredulous wonder. One of his co-writers on the show *Seinfeld* says that if Seinfeld were a superhero he would be Microscope Man.

Of course, Seinfeld does have extraordinary powers. He kills us, not with lightning bolts or superhuman strength, but with laughter. And he has been killing us for seventeen years, first in small comedy clubs, then on guest appearances on *The Tonight Show* and *Late Night with David Letterman*. Now he is the co-creator, sometime writer, and star of his own phenomenally successful situation comedy on NBC.

On the show Seinfeld plays himself, a single man living in New York, surrounded by three passionately neurotic friends. *Seinfeld* eerily mimics the life of its star and the show's other writers, until it seems sometimes that there is little difference between life and art. The show was an underground hit in its first seasons but only won a big audience during 1992–93. Probably the largest audience ever to see it so far — 20 million people — tuned into the season's final episode, in which the TV Jerry (as the people who work on the show call Seinfeld's character) actually filmed *his* own television pilot. There was a nice moment during the episode, one of those small touches that the show is famous for, in which Jerry's ex-girlfriend Elaine is sitting in a restaurant with the head of NBC who just happens to be crazy about her. When the NBC head mentions the new show starring Jerry Seinfeld that the network is going to air, Elaine pretends not to know Jerry personally. "He's that, 'Did you ever notice this, did you ever notice that' guy," she deadpans.

In a way, yes, that is what Seinfeld the comic does. He notices something. He finds it peculiar. Then he puts it under his microscope and blows it up larger so that the rest of us who aren't as blessed with the same vision can see it too. For example, here is his questioning of the purpose of McDonald's continuing to count the number of hamburgers sold. "What are they up to, 80 billion?" he asks. "What is their goal? To have cows surrendering voluntarily?"

But Seinfeld did not always feel as invincible as Thor when he stood before an audience. On his first-ever attempt at stand-up comedy, when he was in his early twenties and just out of college, Seinfeld walked onto the stage at Catch a Rising Star in New York during an open-mike night. And froze. He managed to name the subjects of his routine: "The beach. Driving. Shopping. Parents." Then he walked off. The MC, Elayne Boosler, took back the microphone and said, "That was Jerry Seinfeld, the king of segues."

Success, however, has finally come to Jerry Seinfeld. Unlike George, his friend on *Seinfeld* who is modeled after his real-life friend Larry David, Seinfeld is not afraid of success. He harbors no secret wish to fail. As he said in the monologue of the 1992 season finale, "To me the whole concept of fear of success means that we are scraping the bottom of the fear barrel." Perhaps Seinfeld has no such fear because success means less to him than it does for other stars, because his is focused not on the result but on the means. He has never desired anything else but to be a consummate comic. Not a talk-show host, like Jay Leno and Whoopi Goldberg, not a film actor like Eddie Murphy and Billy Crystal, not even the star of a situation comedy. Indeed, his first television acting job was such a disaster that he fled back to the comedy stage.

"I remember some comedian in a book saying, 'You don't want to be fifty years old getting up on a Tuesday night in Milwaukee,'" he once told *New York*. "Yes, I do. that's exactly what I want to do."

Oh yes, there's also the Zen. The Zen helps too.

Jerry's childhood home in Massapequa, on Long Island.

When we are children we see with a clarity that we later lose as adults. Perhaps it's because as children we have our faces so closely pressed to life: to the grass where the insects are, to the window of our parents' car, to the back of the cereal box. Seinfeld still has his face pressed close to life.

Take that cereal. Most adults, if they haven't given up eating cereal in the morning, spoon it down while reading the morning paper. But Seinfeld can still see this morning ritual with a child's precision. "Milk-estimation skills — so important," he tells the audience. "What do you do when you get to the bottom of the bowl and you still have milk left? I say, put in more cereal!" Seinfeld himself likes to try every new gimmicky cereal that comes on the market, and he likes to mix three or four kinds at a time in a bowl so large he calls it his "Jethro bowl." He once mentioned to *USA Today* that he had eaten some Trix that morning. "I hadn't done that in quite some time. I made myself sick eating it. To me, eating Trix is like doing heroin, it's something you know you're not supposed to be doing. It's really misbehaving." Carol Leifer, a comic who Seinfeld dated in the late seventies, told the newspaper, "He's the cereal god. Even if you weren't into cereal, you eat cereal with Jerry because there's no way of escaping it. It's all over his place." This is not just an eccentricity; it's a part of childhood that Seinfeld won't let go of.

The child's view can be seen in many of Seinfeld's routines, even when he presents them as the perspective of an adult. One of the comics he most admires and learned his technique from is Bill Cosby, whose most brilliant routines of the late 1960s and early 1970s used kid characters such as Fat Albert. As a teenager, Seinfeld played Cosby's records over and over, memorizing the routines and learning his timing. Cosby's influence can be seen in some of Seinfeld's material about children. In one bit, Seinfeld pretends to be a little kid being dragged around to stores by his mother. The kid is so bored that he has to lie down on the floor — right in the middle of a bank. No matter how hard his mother hauls on his arm, the kid refuses to rise. "I cannn't get up," whines Seinfeld the kid. "It's toooo dull in here." In another he waxes lyrical about the joys of a cardboard refrigerator box. "When you're five that's the closest you're going to come to having your own apartment."

Jerome Seinfeld was born on April 29, 1954, in Brooklyn, New York. New York seems to be a comic breeding ground, as if there were something in the water, although Seinfeld's family soon moved to Massapequa, on Long Island. (He likes to explain that Massapequa is "an old Indian name that means 'By the Mall.'") Both his mother and father had been raised without their own real parents, and as a consequence were highly independent people — a trait they passed onto Jerry.

Seinfeld's father, Kalman, owned a commercial sign-painting business, doing the painting himself. He had a locally famous sense of humor and the young Jerry was impressed with his power to make people laugh. "My dad was very funny," he told *People*. "He turned me on that it's fun to be funny. That's why I really do it." Another time he said, "I watched the effect he would have on people, and I thought that was for me." Even today, some people who knew him insist that Kalman was the funniest Seinfeld ever.

Seinfeld's mother, Betty, ran the household. She recognized early that her son had a large and ambitious appetite. "He never wanted just a piece of cake. It was the whole cake," she informed *People*. She calls him "Mr. Perfection" because of his finicky insistence that everything be just right, and just the way *he* wants it. Seinfeld's sister, Carolyn, who is 18 months older, agrees. His personality as a child was much the same as it is now, she says. He was always a driven and obsessive person.

Kalman died in 1985, and while he never saw the show *Seinfeld*, he did live long enough to see his son rise to prominence as a stand-up comic who appeared frequently on television. Betty, now in her late seventies, lives in a retirement community in Delray Beach, Florida. She has a bedroom in her condominium apartment reserved for her son when he visits. No doubt Seinfeld found it a short step to acting the episode of *Seinfeld* in which Jerry and Elaine visit Jerry's parents in Florida. For that show's monologue he used one of the best jokes of his stand-up routine: "My folks just moved to Florida this past year. They didn't want to move to Florida but they're in their sixties and that's the law."

Young Jerry's suburban upbringing was by all accounts happy and normal. He was a cute kid, with regular features, that same slightly pointed chin, a high forehead, and rather big ears. One photograph taken when he was about eight shows him as the quintessential American boy, with the upper front teeth missing.

But ordinary Jerry was not so ordinary inside. "I may look meek and mild," he told *Playboy*, "but inside there's a raging superpower. Superman in my mind was, and still is, the ultimate guy, the role I was born to play." (In fact he did play the role many years later, in a sketch on *Saturday Night Live*.) Seinfeld discovered how to let his superpower out when he was eight years old and watched *The Ed Sullivan Show* one Sunday night. For years America tuned in every week to this variety show which was a showcase for a wide assortment of acts. Watching it, Seinfeld saw his first comic perform — and get laughs. Soon he was scouring the television listings to find other comics to watch. He kept this early passion a secret, not even confiding it to his parents or his sister. Later he would continue to keep it a secret from them even after he had started to perform in clubs.

"I knew I was going to be a comedian at a very young age,"

Massapequa High School.

Jerry's high-school graduation picture.

Seinfeld has said. "I remember one time I made a friend laugh so hard he sprayed a mouthful of cookies and milk all over me, and I liked it. That was the beginning."

At the age of 13 or 14, Seinfeld started tape-recording comic interviews with his pet parakeet. Perhaps the bird was the inspiration for a routine of the 1980s about the tendency of pet parakeets to fly into mirrors. "Even if he thinks the mirror is another room, why doesn't he avoid hitting the other parakeet?"

He was not a gregarious child, nor particularly popular. Seinfeld told *GQ*, "When you retreat from contact with other kids, your only playground left is your own mind. You start exploring your ability to entertain yourself." While funny as a kid, he wasn't a show-off, or a trouble-maker either for that matter. Even then he liked to be well-groomed and neat in appearance.

Early on he became a television addict and his mother bemoaned this apparent waste of time. "Jerry was *chained* to the television," she remembered in *Playboy*. But that early watching was a kind of training for the comic-to-be. Seinfeld learned some of his style and the way to find material in the most common things from television. He himself swears to this day that he learned most of what he knows about life from the tube.

At Massapequa High School Seinfeld wasn't the class cut-up, but he was something of a wise-guy, sitting in the back of class and making jokes under his breath. He wasn't an especially popular kid then either, or one with a lot of friends. He did like to entertain his fellow students by repeating jokes from *Rowan and Martin's Laugh-In*, doing routines off George Carlin records, and imitating Yogi Bear. (That may have been Seinfeld's only imitation. Unlike many other comics, he doesn't do voices.) Seinfeld graduated from Massapequa High in 1972, an event that he enshrined in his joke about renting a tuxedo.

Queen's College, Flushing, New York.

RHONDA SEIDMAN

JERRY SEINFELD
THEATRE / MASS
COMMUNICATIONS
Dean's List

Jerry's college graduation picture.

"There's a thrill — wearing a suit that's already been worn by 80 high school guys on the most exciting night their glands have ever known."

THE INTERROGATION ROOM

Seinfeld enrolled at Queens College, in Flushing, New York, and studied for a double major in theater and communication arts. He was five feet eleven inches, slight of build, and looked even younger than he was. (Even today he looks five or six years younger than his age.) In 1976 he graduated with a bachelor of arts and even made the dean's list. "I never felt my college years were wasted," he asserted to the *Chicago Tribune*. "Comedy is communicating, after all." But Seinfeld's mind was already elsewhere.

On the same day as graduation, he took to the stage of Catch a Rising Star, the city's premiere comedy club, where stage fright prevented him from getting out the material he'd written. "I got up there, the bright lights hit my face, I'd never touched a microphone, and I froze solid," he recalled to *New York Newsday*. But for some reason the audience found his presence amusing and tittered at the few disjointed words that he did manage to squeak out.

A few friends who came to witness this inauguration assured Seinfeld that the audience had seen something in him, and he felt encouraged enough to try a second time. Despite not having used the first routine, he wrote all new material and took it to the Golden Lion Pub. At the time comedy clubs were just beginning their rise to enormous popularity. Unlike Catch a Rising Star, the Golden Lion was a modest eating and drinking place. At night a stage was made simply by removing one table. Overhead a single lightbulb burned, "like an interrogation room," Seinfeld remembered.

Even to get this inauspicious start, Seinfeld had to audition for the owner one lunch hour, with a single diner as his audience. Fortunately he passed the test and went on to perform for several months. The first laugh he ever got was for a bit about his being left-handed and the way society views everything left in a negative way. "Two left feet . . . they left, stuff like that," he told *USA Today*. "That was my first stage laugh." It isn't much of a stretch to say that his material has improved considerably since then. Only after a while did he tell his family about his entry into show business. "I think they just assumed it was a phase I was going through, and I'd get over it and get into a real career," he remarked to the *Chicago Tribune*.

Performers are always hoping to be spotted by a bigshot in the business — it's one of the enduring Hollywood clichés. One night Jackie Mason came to the Golden Lion and caught Seinfeld's act. Mason's style was completely different from the young comic's. With his heavy-tongued accent and broad *shtick* on the differences between Jews and gentiles, Mason was a holdover from the era of "borscht-belt" comedians who used to entertain guests at Catskill resorts. Seinfeld, on the other hand, was a thoroughly assimilated American who never directly touched on his Jewishness. Still, to a sensitive ear there was something Jewish about Seinfeld's pin-point observations, his crankiness when confronted with life's idiocies.

Mason stayed to the end of the show so that he could introduce himself to a thrilled Seinfeld and lavish him with encouragement. Later he told the *New York Times* what he had seen in the young comic. "He had a great natural comedy style — an ingratiating quality. His humor was founded on basic truths and universal subjects."

Mason wasn't the only famous comic to discover Seinfeld early. Rodney Dangerfield did too. In September 1976 Danger-field hosted a special for the Home Box Office channel called

Rodney Dangerfield — It's Not Easy Bein' Me. Dangerfield himself only introduced the show and performed in a few skits along with a young female comedian named Roseanne Barr who acted as his frumpy wife. The rest of the show was devoted to new comics. The pay-TV channels had found comics a good and inexpensive source of programming that appealed to the same young adults who frequented the clubs but which the networks had left largely untapped. Just months after his start as a stand-up, Seinfeld had a spot on the special. He was picked out of the line-up by the *Washington Post* critic, Tom Shales. Shales singled out "droll mellow fellow Jerry Seinfeld, one of the brightest yet least flashy of working comics." The critic liked Seinfeld's observational style and noted that his clean act was a refreshing contrast to so many comics who used obscenities to get easy laughs or talked only about sex.

While Shales' praise would be echoed by other critics in the future, at the time the special did not boost Seinfeld to stardom. He remained a little-known comic and an inexperienced one, with little first-rate material in his repertoire. As he told the *New York Times*, "I think it takes five years just to learn how to express yourself, to know what to say." He also had to find his own stage presence, which in Seinfeld's case was as close to his real self as possible. "I find that the best stage persona is the one that's closest to your real personality. You can live with that and do it for years," he contended in the *Boston Globe*. Besides the Golden Lion Pub (which has since ceased to exist), he started to perform at other New York venues, including the Improvisation, the Comic Strip, Garvins, and the Cellar Door. To save money he lived on club hamburgers, wore club t-shirts, and gave up wearing socks and a belt.

Before long Seinfeld was venturing a little farther afield. He was only 22 when he got his first gig playing a big room at a Catskill hotel. Unfortunately, he bombed. "Total silence," Seinfeld recalled with pain. "And in a big room, you feel like you're just falling through space." Almost just as bad was opening for other acts in Las Vegas, when his job was to warm up the audience for the main attraction. "The toughest nights were opening for these real old-time Italian singers. I'm like Grace Jones to them. 'This guy is nuts — talking about socks! Where's the wife jokes, where's the fat jokes?' "

In the late seventies, Seinfeld wore his fuzzy hair higher and longer than now, along with large glasses, and performed in a shirt open at the neck and with wide lapels. On a good night he was paid 30 or 50 dollars, but just as often he performed for nothing. For four years he worked almost every night, rarely taking a day off. When he wasn't performing he was hanging out in the clubs, meeting other comics and watching their acts. Because of the fewer number of clubs then it was possible to see virtually everyone doing stand-up. He and his fellow comics would spend the night in the clubs from 9 p.m. until about 1 a.m. and then would head to a coffee shop where they would sit talking until 4 in the morning. It was an intense period of learning, performing, failing, and succeeding — a comic boot-camp.

NOTHING TO FALL BACK ON

Even someone living frugally couldn't survive on what Seinfeld made at the clubs. During the years from 1976 until 1980 he also held a series of menial jobs to keep body and soul together. One of them was selling long-life bulbs by telephone. "Tough job," he joked. "There's not many people sitting at home, saying, 'I'm here in the dark. I can't hold out much longer.' "

He also worked as a waiter in a luncheonette, swept floors in a film-editing studio, and even worked as an unlicensed peddlar, selling costume jewelry from a cart outside of

Bloomingdales. "Running from the police on the streets of Manhattan — this is a parents' dream come true."

But if the jobs were lousy, they were *deliberately* lousy. Seinfeld took the worst positions he could find; his odd but logical thinking was that they would force him to succeed as a comic. He told *Entertainment Weekly*, "To have your back to a cliff, that's the best way to accomplish something. Never have anything to fall back on."

It was at this time, not long after graduating from college, that Seinfeld enrolled in a couple of Scientology courses. Begun in the 1950s by science-fiction writer L. Ron Hubbard, Scientology is part religion, part pseudo-science, part therapy, and has a following around the world. It has generated a great deal of controversy with accusers calling it a cult and a system for swindling followers out of their assets. Governments have prosecuted Scientology for tax evasion and other offenses.

From an early age Seinfeld showed himself to be a person with a need to feel in control of his surroundings, his life, his relationships, and his work. That need is one of the motivating factors in his passion for stand-up comedy, in which he can be both writer and performer, without having to rely on anyone else. Seinfeld admits abhorring even the idea of depending on another person. Since becoming an adult he has searched to find a larger approach to life that would help him in this need, that would increase his sense of confidence, serenity, control, and acceptance of life. While he took only those first courses and did not continue as a member afterwards, Seinfeld credits Scientology with teaching him a lot about ethics, relationships, self-discipline, and self-reliance.

Despite the fact that this dabbling took place years ago, Seinfeld's interest in Scientology has come back to haunt him now that he is a celebrity. In 1992 Roseanne Arnold (formerly Barr), star of ABC's number one hit show *Roseanne*, and her husband Tom Arnold publicly brought up the issue of

Seinfeld's relationship to Scientology. Roseanne Arnold told the *Washington Post*, "You can see it reflected in the kind of comedy he does." The response of most Seinfeld fans to that accusation can only be *huh*? Perhaps Roseanne Arnold, not the most emotionally secure of comics, felt threatened by the rise of *Seinfeld* in the ratings and the critical praise being heaped on the show. Seinfeld himself has mused aloud about the contrast to his relatively happy and uneventful upbringing and Roseanne's traumatic one, which she has talked about endlessly on talk shows.

Whatever the reason, Seinfeld felt the need to defend his past. He said that his interest in Scientology was akin to his interest in Eastern religions which he has also studied, and that he has simply taken from it what was useful to him. "I was never in the organization," he asserted to the *Washington Post*. "I don't represent them in any way." However, he did feel compelled to denounce a cover story in *Time* that attacked Scientology as a cult greedy for power and wealth.

That was not the end of the war that the Arnolds seem to have declared on Seinfeld. In spring 1992 Julia Louis-Dreyfus, who plays Elaine on *Seinfeld*, was instructed to park her car in the spot reserved for Tom Arnold on the Studio City lot. But when she returned, Louis-Dreyfus found an obscene note on her car. Even though she stopped parking there, other notes followed, along with a Polaroid photograph of a hefty set of naked buttocks. While Roseanne offered a weak apology, she also called Louis-Dreyfus a "bitch" on *Late Night with David Letterman*. If this wasn't enough, Roseanne felt the need to trash the show for trying to be different from most of network television. "They think they're doing Samuel Beckett instead of a sitcom," she sneered. The other cast members were angry and protective of Louis-Dreyfus, but were ordered not to talk to the press. In Hollywood, it isn't just crazed fans that celebrities have to worry about.

2

Welcome to L.A.

After four years of performing in the clubs, Seinfeld believed that he had 25 minutes of good material. But he wasn't advancing very quickly and decided that, despite his love for New York — the only city where he felt really at home — he had to move to Los Angeles for the sake of his career.

Los Angeles: city of smog, highways, skateboards, and incredible tans. Of would-be stars, high-powered agents, unproduced screenwriters. And of real celebrities who table hop at Spago to schmooze with other real celebrities. But Seinfeld could hardly afford an appetizer at Spago, let alone a meal; Los Angeles turned out to be an even harder place to survive than New York. At night he performed in the local clubs while during the day he auditioned fruitlessly for roles on television shows. These casting sessions are, to say the least, unpleasant experiences for an actor. He must sit for long periods in rooms crowded with other actors auditioning for the same part. Then he is brought into a room where he has to talk about his recent work before a group of edgy producers, writers, the director, and network executives. Finally he reads a few pages of a script while they scrutinize him. Almost invariably the result is rejection.

In retrospect it was a strange move for somebody wanting

to be a comic and who admitted to having the most limited acting skills. But other comics had made it to television, a few succeeding if even more crashed and burned. For better or worse, it must have seemed the inevitable route to follow.

Pretty soon Seinfeld was broke and with no means of supporting himself. One night, down to his last 20 dollars, he performed at a local club. In the audience was a casting agent who recognized a new talent and got Seinfeld an audition for a part that was opening on the sitcom, *Benson*. A spin-off from the show *Soap*, *Benson* concerned a black butler (played by Robert Guillaume) who worked for an American governor named James Gatling (played by James Noble). The show first aired in 1979 and would have a successful run until 1986.

Seinfeld auditioned and won the part. Not a very big part, mind you. He was cast as Frankie, a joke writer for the governor who was meant to be a less than useful addition to his staff. Seinfeld appeared on the show during the 1980–81 season and was paid $4,000 an episode — not much by television standards but a king's fortune to a guy with 20 bucks in his pocket.

In one scene from *Benson*, Frankie is dressed like a teenager — which is about as old as Seinfeld looks — in a t-shirt and hooded sweatshirt. Seinfeld is very thin and has his hair parted in the middle. The scene takes place in the kitchen where Frankie is trying out a new joke for the governor on Benson. Frankie says, "Did you hear about the rabbi who bought himself a ranch? Called it the Bar Mitzvah." Frankie laughs inanely, but Benson replies only with a look of disgust. Disappointed, Frankie asks, "Too Jewish? Too western?"

Delivering his lines broadly, Seinfeld weaves back and forth with misplaced energy, a stark contrast to his demeanor on *Seinfeld* where he often stands perfectly still. Seinfeld had nothing to do with the scripts of *Benson* and believed that it was a dumb idea to expect people to laugh at a character who delivered bad jokes. Apparently the show's producers agreed with him; they fired Seinfeld after three episodes.

To this day Seinfeld resents the way he was treated on the show. One day he arrived at rehearsal as usual and sat down at the table for the initial read-through of the script. Only there was no copy of the script for him. The assistant director called him aside and said that they had neglected to inform him that, ah, he wasn't on the show any more. No explanation was offered.

Not only was getting fired so casually a humiliating experience, but it made the whole *Benson* moment seem over before it had begun. "It happened so fast, it was like a car accident," Seinfeld said. Without question this was one of the lowest points of his career. What hurt the most, though, was Seinfeld's disappointment with himself. What had happened to his love and dedication to stand-up comedy? He had wasted his time auditioning for puerile television roles when he could have been working on new routines and improving his style. But Seinfeld wasn't defeated. He had only been temporarily sidetracked, and could turn this failure into an opportunity to rededicate himself to the art of stand-up. Seinfeld vowed never again to give up so much control of his career to people around him. If he ever did another television show, he would have to be the star.

Today when a rerun of *Benson* with Frankie the joke writer is aired, Seinfeld feels only a deep embarrassment. He can take comfort in knowing that he kept to his vow — to the letter.

THE ART OF STAND-UP

From 1980 onwards, Seinfeld concentrated on developing more material and honing its delivery before live audiences at the comedy clubs. While his basic style had been there almost from the beginning, he refined it until he eventually became the reigning master of recognition humor.

Actually, recognition humor is hardly new. At one time it was called observational humor: the comic, noting small everyday aspects of life, comments on them in an amusing way. But the term "recognition" brings in a crucial aspect of what makes Seinfeld funny to so many people. The audience recognizes what he is talking about, it is a part of *their* lives too, only they have never really thought about it before. When Seinfeld presents it to them the absurdity is magnified so that everyone can see it. The result is a laugh, not just because it's funny, but because we share in the observation. While some comics thrive on hostility, recognition is a bond that links Seinfeld to his audience in a friendly relationship.

Take his comment about dry cleaning, something few of us have consciously thought about. "What the hell *is* dry cleaning fluid?" Seinfeld wonders aloud. "It's not a fluid if it's dry." Only now does the audience realize that they, too, have no idea how dry cleaning actually cleans their clothes. Or take his comment on soap-on-a-rope. "That comes in handy. Sometimes I'm in the shower I want to hang myself." Or his rumination on why only the father of the house is allowed to touch the thermostat. "I don't think I touched a thermostat until I was 28 years old."

Seinfeld wouldn't be offended to hear that he hasn't invented this form of humor. He has compared comedy to a suit; the lapels might be wider or narrower, but a suit is always a suit. His is a classical approach to comedy, that puts him into the long line of mainstream comics along with Bob Hope and Jay Leno. You don't need a college degree to get his jokes, like Woody Allen, or to be a member of an ethnic group. There's no need for obscenities or denigrations of women, religious or cultural groups — although even if there was, Seinfeld wouldn't do them. "Maybe it just reflects me in some way, but

Jerry performing stand-up .

that's always been one of the challenges in comedy, to do something positive," he told *Ladies Home Journal*.

Some comics, like Robin Williams, are more manic performers, offering a series of emotional and theatrical highs and lows. Seinfeld isn't like that; he's never outrageous and no one moment of his act stands out above all the rest. He has no gimmick, like screaming the same line over and over or wearing bizarre clothing or an arrow through his head. He does no imitations, plays no characters other than himself. Instead, he presents us with Jerry Seinfeld, a good-natured if somewhat cynical young man who can't help wondering about those little details that make up modern life. His material has a consistently high quality and during the 1980s he learned to deliver it with increasing confidence, panache, and grace.

There was another aspect to performing that Seinfeld also had to learn — understanding the audience. "Solving audiences is a big part of being a comedian," Seinfeld explained to the *Los Angeles Times*. "An audience is a very tricky thing. A laugh is not just a laugh. It has different breadth and different amplitude and different pitch. And you learn to interpret what those things mean." Often Seinfeld would open with a few of his staple jokes, in order to judge the response. Some audiences, for example, became uncomfortable when he made fun of people, while others lapped it up. A cold audience might respond only mildly to even his best material, while a hot audience that was eager to laugh was perfect for trying new material and stretching jokes as far as they could go.

Without a gimmick or catch-line, Seinfeld's recognition was a matter of slow growth rather than being meteoric. One television appearance couldn't make him a star, as it did Steven Wright. On the other hand, Wright has faded quickly because of the limitations of his act. Jay Leno, who replaced Johnny Carson as host of *The Tonight Show*, is a comic whose style shares similarities with Seinfeld's. Leno too is a seemingly ordinary, decent, and likeable guy who happens to say funny things. (A major difference is that Leno is sometimes a political comic, who is not afraid to be razzed by the *Tonight Show* audience for taking a verbal shot at the president. The closest Seinfeld gets to politics is his comment on the civil service: "Watching postal employees is like watching a lava lamp.") Leno told *Playboy*, "By being a normal person who is a funny guy, Jerry has to do 20 appearances to only one the guy who is outrageous and strange has to do."

Leno and Seinfeld are actually good friends, which isn't surprising since comics like to hang out together and help each other on their acts. Leno often kids his friend about their being similar kinds of comics, while Seinfeld likes to pretend they have nothing at all in common. But Seinfeld does concede that when Leno took over *The Tonight Show* he opened a space for another "normal" funny guy to come up behind him.

HEEERE'S JERRY

Not long after the *Benson* disaster, Seinfeld was busy performing again. But he wasn't any better known; rather, he was just one of the countless aspiring comics warming up the club audience before the headline act. Then another break came his way — came, like the others, because of the quality of his work. Seinfeld was performing in a Los Angeles club and among the audience that night was a talent scout for none other than *The Tonight Show*. The scout booked him for an appearance and suddenly Seinfeld had the chance that every comic hopes for. He had just turned 30.

Under Johnny Carson, himself a comic, *The Tonight Show* was every comedian's dream gig. Many comedians had been lifted from the obscurity of the clubs to national prominence after an appearance on the show. Many more of course had not fulfilled the scout's original assessment and had never returned. Seinfeld was both hopeful and terrified. "So here I had five years of going out every night and developing my act, and I was going to take all the chips I'd developed and put them into the center of the table on one five-minute bit," Seinfeld remembered for the *New York Times*. Meanwhile, his proud father Kalman painted a sign and mounted it on his van: "JERRY'S ON CARSON TONIGHT." It was May 7, 1981. "Every comedian knows that date — their own, I mean," Seinfeld said.

This time Seinfeld did not freeze under the lights as he had at his first try at Catch a Rising Star. The audience liked him and, just as important for making it in the business, Johnny Carson did too. "Suddenly," Seinfeld told the *Times*, "I was lifted from the pack in L.A."

While the appearance did not make him a national celebrity, it did turn him into a headliner in the comedy clubs, the guy that the audience comes to see and for whom the other comics are the lead up. Naturally, his fee for performing increased too. After that first time, Seinfeld became a semi-regular on the show and has appeared on it more than 25 times. With each performance his profile went up a notch and the number of Seinfeld admirers increased. It may be more than a coincidence that the show airs on NBC, the network that would eventually approach the comic with an offer that would result in *Seinfeld*.

Even after he became well known, Seinfeld never took his *Tonight Show* dates for granted. After all, those millions of viewers were potential audience members of his stand-up act whenever he toured the country. The short time allowed on the show doesn't permit many mistakes — one dud line can sour a performance. For a 1990 appearance, for example, Seinfeld tried out his material at the Improv, *the* comedy club in Los Angeles, while a fellow comedian named Jimmy Brogan timed him with a watch. Despite being rivals, comics have a strong sense of camaraderie. Seinfeld has helped his friends prepare acts too and once when he was on tour he flew back to Los Angeles to give moral support to a friend who was making his first *Tonight Show* appearance.

The year after Seinfeld first made it onto Carson's show, another important television venue for comics made its debut: *Late Night with David Letterman*. With a time-slot on NBC following *The Tonight Show*, it quickly developed a hip, young audience who enjoyed Letterman's off-centered, cynical, deliberately juvenile and sometimes nasty humor. Despite his friendship with Jay Leno who has taken over from Johnny Carson, Seinfeld praises *Late Night* (renamed *Late Show* after moving to CBS) for being the best talk show on television. But he names both Leno and Letterman among his personal favorite comics, along with Robert Klein and Larry Miller. Seinfeld quickly became a regular guest on *Late Night* too, increasing his audience even more and proving that he could have a wide appeal.

*Arriving at Los Angeles International Airport
from New York City, July 8, 1990.*

3

The Coolest Thing on the Planet

Seinfeld's appearances on television (he was also a guest 18 times on the now-defunct *Merv Griffin Show*) certainly helped raise him to national attention, but his real work was before live audiences. During the eighties he began to play more and more cities, until he was doing an astonishing 300 performances a year, criss-crossing the country and logging 300,000 air miles annually. As he remarked to the *Washington Post*, "I walk through airports for a living." He also found a joke in those bored airport employees who run the x-ray machines — "a crack squad of savvy, motivated individuals."

By 1987 Seinfeld was being called one of America's most outstanding comedians by *Time*. (His friend Leno was still "king of the stand-up circuit.") In another *Time* article, Richard Zoglin called him "the quintessential yuppie comic of the '80s" for his "laid-back observations about the trivial pursuits of modern life. . . ." Seinfeld was coming to be identified as a kind of comic spokesman for his time and generation.

Recognition began to come in other forms. The American Comedy Awards named him the Funniest Male Stand-Up Comic of 1988, and in the same year he was voted best male comedy-club performer in an audience poll. If Jerry Seinfeld had been a stock, he would have been one of the hottest investments going.

On the simplest level it is easy to understand why audiences began to love Seinfeld; he made them laugh. But why did Seinfeld love stand-up so much? "It's a life mission for me," he confided to *Playboy*. "I don't know what the hell I'm trying to accomplish, but I can't stop."

Certainly it has something to do with his ability to control all aspects of the art and career, especially the writing and performing. The fact that he uses no props, visual aids, music, or other diversions means that he has only his wit to keep the audience's attention. That nakedness makes the performance an absolutely immediate experience for the comic. "Stand-up is the purest performing relation, and there's just nothing else that I have ever done that compares with it," he told *Ladies Home Journal*. He went on to compare it to acting, which to a certain degree can be faked by a non-actor like himself. "Stand-up is a very specific craft, not unlike playing the saxophone. If you don't know how, forget it."

Seinfeld believes that no matter how famous a comic becomes, he can never really be a star the way an actor is. And the biggest mistake for a comic is ever to *believe* that he is a star. No matter how tall your name stands on the marquee, stand-up remains a "grimy gig." Seinfeld has said, "The audience will give you a free ride for five, maybe ten minutes. That's it. If you're not funny that night, I don't care how famous you are. It doesn't matter. As long as I'm doing my stand-up, the audience will keep me in my place."

Being on stage is a kind of existential experience for Seinfeld, making him feel life most fully and directly. Too often we feel as if we are only half alive, not completely aware of ourselves, of time passing, of our environment. But standing before an audience making them laugh is for Seinfeld "an authentic moment in your life." And one that he will never grow bored of because he will never meet all its challenges. "You have to know how far you can get," he mused to the *New York Times*. "Something that hasn't been done. And there is no one else who can do it — because no one else can do *you*."

In trying to describe the feeling of creating a great joke, Seinfeld told *Playboy*, "I'd rather say something that people would quote as a great line that I said, that I *thought* of, than win an Oscar." He recounted a story. "I was in a car going from Philadelphia to New York, at one o'clock in the morning, listening to the radio. It was the postgame show for the Dodgers game when Kirk Gibson hit that homer. And the guy quoted me as he described what a great day in sports it had been. He said, 'It's like Jerry Seinfeld says, how are we ever going to impress our kids? What stories will we have? How can the world change that much again that we can blow kids away with stories like the ones our parents told us, about the war and the Depression, when milk was a nickel and cars were a quarter? What will we say? *When I was a boy, dogs didn't have the vote. They had no say in the world at all, in fact, we kept them on leashes.*' When I heard that on the radio, that was the biggest boost I'd ever had. That, to me, is the coolest thing you could do on this planet."

A lot of comedians complain about life on the road — the endless plane and bus trips, the lonely hotel rooms, the bad food. Seinfeld, however, liked touring, which seemed inseparable from being a stand-up comic. In his overactive mind which had retained the imaginative capacity of childhood he thought of himself as "the assassin," moving alone, with only a flight bag, cool and independent and dangerous. The bag contained a nice suit and fashionable tie; no more open shirts for him, although he did become known for the white Nike running shoes he liked to wear. Seinfeld ruminated in *Playboy* about the countless airline flights that drive others to distraction: "What am I doing on these flights? I'm reading a magazine. I'm saying, 'Yes, I think I will have lemon with that club soda.' Does this really wear people down? . . . I enjoy all these trappings — the airports, the smoke in my face, the humiliating dressing rooms. It means I'm a comic."

Seinfeld's contentment with himself and desire to be in control of his own life made all those empty hotel rooms easier to bear. Unlike some, he had no spouse and kids to miss back home, and his career took precedence over any relationship that he happened to be involved in. (Not surprisingly, those relationships didn't last long.) Seinfeld was happy enough to occupy himself by leaning on the bed writing new jokes with a Bic pen on a yellow legal pad. He was a disciplined writer and could write jokes for one or two hours, however long he set for himself. It didn't make the life any harder that as he began to play larger venues his income began to rise considerably. In 1988 he played the Cascade Showroom at Caesar's Tahoe and his take was in the five figures. Comedy was starting to become serious business.

THE CONFIDENTIAL COMIC

Television and comedy has been a natural match from Milton Berle and Sid Caesar onwards, but only in recent years have comics been able to transfer their acts directly to the small screen. The pay-TV channel Home Box Office was a leader in using comics and began a series of specials that were essentially tapings of live performances. In 1987 HBO tapped Seinfeld on the shoulder and the result was *Jerry Seinfeld: Stand-Up Confidential*, which first aired in September 1987. (It was released on video only after NBC's *Seinfeld* had its first summer season almost three years later.)

The special's executive producers were Seinfeld's manager, George Shapiro, and Howard West (who would also become a manager for Seinfeld), and the director was Bruce Gowers. The production values were, to put it kindly, meager, and the direction lacked an intimacy that would have put Seinfeld over most strongly to a television audience. The rhythm of the show was broken up by the intercutting of a series of skits meant to extend it to a full hour. Even so, Seinfeld's best routines shine though.

Carl Reiner, another great comic from the previous generation who recognized Seinfeld's talent, introduces him to the Los Angeles audience before whom the program was taped. Then Seinfeld bounces on, looking remarkably young, his face thin and pointed, his eyebrows arched. He wears a dark suit, thin tie, and good shoes — no Nike runners this time. While performing he paces from one end of the stage to the other to play to the whole audience and uses his lean body and narrow hands for effect.

While none of Seinfeld's routines are long — many are only a couple of lines — he sometimes strings together related material. The special's main theme is the family. He moans about family gatherings where, no matter what the subject under discussion, someone always ends by sighing, "Well, what are you going to do?" (Seinfeld's intonation is the closest he gets to Jewish content.) There is a great bit on the way fathers make a big deal out of moving furniture and another on how they insist on packing the trunk of the car themselves before trip: "It goes in some special way that only I understand." Although Jerry talks about his own father, in fact Kalman Seinfeld had died two years before. Comics often fictionalize their families this way, although one wonders what kind of personal pain is involved.

There is also a charming routine about how a dog feels to be riding in the front of a car — "the ultimate dog experience." Near the end of the act, the jokes change direction more quickly. Seinfeld even throws in some food jokes: "For Oscar

Meyer to come up with a new product he has to invent meat."

The skits on the special, co-written by Joel Hodgson, are for the most part weak, and a few are embarrassingly bad. Only one is really funny. Seinfeld plays a teacher instructing a class of young students how to understand their fathers. He translates father-speak for them: "I'm gonna watch a little TV" really means "I'm gonna fall asleep in a chair." But the skits are interesting for another reason; in them can be seen the germ of the idea that will later become the television show *Seinfeld*.

In the first skit Seinfeld, speaking to the camera, says that people often ask him where his material comes from. So he is providing each viewer with a pair of x-ray glasses that will allow him or her to see life the way a comic does. The premise of *Seinfeld* would be the same: to show how a comic turns real-life situations into stand-up routines. One of the skits on the HBO special has Jerry as a kid listening to the family argue pointlessly, just like Jerry's parents on the future television show.

John O'Connor, the *New York Times* critic, gave the special a decidedly mixed review. While noting that the skits fell flat, he made an observation more shrewd than he could know. O'Connor wrote, "The engaging comic and the struggling actor keep cancelling each other out." Not until *Seinfeld* would the two merge together.

HOW TO BE FAMOUS

In the late eighties, Seinfeld was a headline act. Articles in newspapers and magazines began to appear — not features or cover stories, but the sort of coverage that marks a performer as the latest discovery for those not yet in the know. But from 1989 to 1990 Seinfeld's career took off like a rocket. He moved from playing intimate comedy clubs for week-long engagements to packing auditoriums, moving to a new city every day or two. The transition seemed so smooth to Seinfeld that he almost didn't realize that something major was happening. He went from earning $1,500 a performance, which wasn't bad for 45 minutes' work, to $17,000.

Seinfeld's career was being helped by increasing television exposure. He appeared again on HBO, this time as a performer at the 1989 *Montreal International Comedy Festival*. And he hosted an NBC special that aired on April 18, 1990, called *Spy Magazine Presents How To Be Famous*.

Spy was a monthly satirical magazine that revelled in exposing the over-privileged lives of the rich and the foolish behavior of the famous. It had an audience of young adults that mirrored Seinfeld's own fans. (Movie aficionados know that the magazine is named after the fictional rag that Jimmy Stewart worked for in *The Philadelphia Story*.) The publishers wanted to branch out into other forms of media and Seinfeld must have seemed to them the perfect host for their first special. Seinfeld was drawn in turn because the project broke the usual network mold — which is one reason it ran at the late hour of 10 p.m. After taping he told the *Washington Post*, "It was a lot of fun to be working with these funny, cynical, New York shut-ins."

Seinfeld acted as host for such scenes as watching people react when a celebrity like Ricardo Montalban walks by. But the special got vicious reviews. *People* called it "tiresome and even cruel," and it was panned by *Variety*, the entertainment industry trade paper, for being "Not a lotta laughs." They were right; the show was dull, grating, and juvenile.

In retrospect, Seinfeld was not a good match for *Spy's* sharp-edged and somewhat sophomoric humor. His own comedy was absurdist rather than satirical and was never really mean-spirited. Fortunately the bad reviews had no effect on Seinfeld's upward climb.

By 1989, Seinfeld's concerts (as comedy acts are more pretentiously called once they moved into larger theatres) had begun to regularly sell out. He practised his trademark recognition humor by commenting on such modern phenomena as the enormous containers of popcorn sold at movie theatres: "I don't need that much roofing insulation." He sold out New York's Town Hall which had 1,500 seats. On the other side of the country, he won over 1,700 fans — more than Bob Hope had drawn there — at the Bren Events Center of the University of California at Irvine. Ten months earlier Seinfeld had played the same town but in a small club. He couldn't help noticing the difference as he stood on the stage looking out at the hall, which looked more like a gymnasium than a theatre. "We won't notice the scoreboard," he ad-libbed, "we'll just pretend it's a little intimate cabaret somewhere on campus." The place rocked with laughter as Seinfeld questioned the wisdom of owning a monkey. "If you need a pet that roller-skates and smokes cigars, it's time to think about a family. You're so close."

After finishing his regular act, Seinfeld returned for an encore of answering questions as he often does. He pretended to read the audience's collective mind: "Let's see how much material he *really* has." (In fact, these days Seinfeld claims to have two hours of first-rate material.) Because questions are often the same from one night to the next, Seinfeld usually has a response at the ready. When asked if he is still single, he answers, "I'm a single guy. I have no other guys attached to me." But sometimes he has to think fast on his feet, a skill learned during all those years in the clubs.

IS FUNNY ENOUGH?

By 1989, Seinfeld was probably the most successful comic on the touring circuit after Jay Leno. The press had begun to move him from the inside pages to feature stories. Seinfeld's manager, George Shapiro, was negotiating with NBC for a television series. Everything seemed to be going right. That is, until the Lawrence Christon review.

Lawrence Christon was the first full-time comedy critic on an American daily newspaper. He had been at the *Los Angeles Times* for more than a decade when he caught Seinfeld's concert at the Bren Center. In his early fifties, he was known to take comedy seriously and to have a rigorous set of personal standards. A comic first had to make Christon laugh to succeed, but that wasn't enough. Great comics, Christon believed, had a depth of meaning and profundity in their material.

The headline on Christon's review of January 17, 1989, was "Laughing on Empty." Christon wrote: "Seinfeld is a pleasant, effortless performer who works clean (no small feat in this time of the howling, offal-heaving monkey). . . . He doesn't traffic in the mindless hate — or self-hate — that characterizes so many other stand-ups. . . . He's expressive. He's clear. And he's completely empty. . . . There isn't a single portion of his act that isn't fun, but ten minutes or so into it, you begin to wonder what this is all about, when is he going to say something or at least come up with something piquant. . . . Seinfeld has no attention span. . . . He has no frame of reference. . . . Seinfeld pays homage to insignificance, and he does it impeccably." According to Christon, Seinfeld had the "bogus sincerity" of a television-commercial pitchman and was "inescapably banal."

To call this a negative review would be an understatement.

Seinfeld tried to shrug off Christon by saying that the audience had loved the show, but it clearly upset him. This criticism — that he was funny but shallow, without any darkness or angst — had trailed him from the beginning of his career and now it rose up to bite. No doubt one of the reasons Seinfeld was so hurt was that it touched a vulnerable place in his armor of self-confidence. Every performer has doubts about his worth and comics can feel especially defensive in a culture that has always considered comedy a lesser form of art than tragedy. Woody Allen is the classic example of a comic who felt that being funny was the artistic equivalent of sitting at the children's table. Would Seinfeld become infected with the same virus? Would he feel the need to be profound too?

Seinfeld was in a somber mood when he talked to *Playboy* about the review. "Christon talked about revealing deeper truths and having social impact, and, yeah, I would love to say great things." He tried to make a distinction between "shallow" (which he hoped he wasn't) and "light" — a real but rather subtle difference. If the problem was that Seinfeld's life was too pleasant and sheltered, well he wasn't going to live a "ragged, desperate existence just so I can talk about that." Perhaps he didn't fully convince himself when he concluded, "I just want to be good."

The simple fact is that Seinfeld is no Dostoevsky. He is not a comic who delves deeply into his own soul to reveal it to the rest of us, or mines the sordid events of his past. He will never be Richard Pryor revealing the horror of cocaine addiction and self-destructiveness. Or Lenny Bruce dissecting the hypocrisies of American society. Seinfeld largely avoids the confessional mode, both because it is not where his natural humor lies and because he feels uneasy dealing with emotion. His best material comes from observations of the world outside, not from the self within.

Seinfeld wasn't the only person upset by the review. His manager, George Shapiro, feared that Christon was such a power in the comedy world that his thumbs down might sink the negotiations with NBC for a series. He responded by sending a slew of favorable reviews of Seinfeld's act to the NBC brass.

A few days later Seinfeld was scheduled to appear on *The Tonight Show*. The show's staff had, of course, read the review and heard the buzz about it, and they were anxious to reassure Seinfeld that he was a real talent. Carl Reiner, another Seinfeld supporter and incidentally also a client of George Shapiro, telephoned to tell Seinfeld how much he disagreed with the review. Seinfeld got up before the *Tonight Show* audience and although he started slow, quickly picked up steam. He slayed the audience with a two-line joke: "Nothing in life is fun for the whole family. There are no massage parlors with ice cream and free jewelry."

In the end, NBC did not lose its faith in Seinfeld and the deal went ahead. But according to *Playboy* Seinfeld fired his manager, George Shapiro, who he felt had somehow not been involved enough in the Christon affair. Seinfeld later relented and re-hired Shapiro.

Like the *Spy* special, the review did not hold back Seinfeld's upward climb. He was simply too funny and too likeable; no matter what a critic said, audiences loved him. A few months later he was able to joke to *Time* just before the premiere of *Seinfeld*, "When you're a shallow person, there's no danger in opening yourself up." But as late as 1992 Seinfeld felt compelled to address this issue of his supposed superficiality. "People complain that my comedy doesn't show a lot of personal anguish, but I look at Laurel and Hardy, you know, and they are my icon of comic perfection," he said to *Ladies Home Journal*. "Something that's so wonderful, and simple to enjoy."

4

Why Is This Man Single?

As Seinfeld's fame grew so did a question in the minds of interviewers and presumably female fans: why is this man single? He soon became one of the country's most famous unattached men when *Cosmopolitan* named him among America's ten most eligible bachelors. The result of that was a deluge of letters from all-too-eligible women.

"Those are the most desirable women," Seinfeld told the *Detroit Free Press* with ironic tongue-in-cheek. "These are the women who sit down and take pictures of themselves with Polaroid Swingers. And then they write letters with crayons in their fist."

Larry David, the co-creator of *Seinfeld*, voiced some concern as Seinfeld's age crept closer to forty. Maybe he was one of those men who had an inability to form a permanent relationship. In fact, Seinfeld *was* engaged once. He was 29 years old, his career was picking up but not yet soaring, and it must have seemed the right time to settle down. But then his thirtieth birthday arrived to shake him up. "Turning 30 just blindsided me," he confided to *People*. "I thought, 'I'd better hurry up and do everything I gotta do.'" He feared that marriage would interfere with his dedication to comedy and, after six months, he broke the engagement off. But he found it hard to do, and he carried guilt feelings long after.

Not so guilty, though, that he couldn't turn the trauma into a comedy routine. Seinfeld told audiences with a rare and candid intensity about his need to break off the engagement. He felt as if he was on a roller coaster just as it was climbing the first hill. How do you get off? "You just say no," he answered himself. "I can't be there. In fact that whole week is bad for me. I've got my Fear of Commitment classes that week, my I Don't Want to Grow Up training seminar is in there."

Seinfeld understood his own Peter Pan syndrome; he still wanted to hang out with the guys, make jokes, and believe that he could fly. But that didn't mean he had to give up an interest in women. He became one of the country's most active daters and seemed to be spotted with a different woman every month. He was attracted to women who were, in his words, "sweet, smart, sexy" and who didn't want him to get dressed up to go out. Only once did he go on a blind date, but he hated the experience — not because of the woman, but because she hadn't been his choice. In romance too Seinfeld didn't like to give up control.

Most of the time the relationships didn't last past the second date, but sometimes they continued long enough for the woman to consider herself Seinfeld's girlfriend, even if he was less committed. Most women found his finickiness hard to live with, an obstacle that even his mother has had to acknowledge with a sigh. After one woman he was seeing took a shower in his West Hollywood condominium, Seinfeld immediately refolded the towel.

Seinfeld has said that he would like to marry and have children, but he confessed to having difficulty making a commitment. His ex-girlfriends, he admitted, would probably describe him as lacking maturity and refusing to accept the demands that a permanent relationship makes on a person. But he made no apologies for putting his career first, especially in these last years when so much has happened for him. "The thing with women," he stated to *New York*, "sometimes I think it bothers them that I have a passion greater than the one I have with them. I'm pretty brutal about my career."

Even if Seinfeld did fall head-over-heals for a woman, he would hardly get to see her given his hectic work schedule. "I'm in this position," he ruefully told the *Detroit Free Press*. "I'm single and successful. But I'm not available. I have nice sports jackets, a nice car. I know where the good restaurants are. But I'm unavailable. It's like I'm married."

In 1991, Seinfeld wrote an article for *Redbook* called "Confessions of an Unromantic Man." Perhaps it came out of a desire to satisfy people's apparent craving to understand his unattached state. He begins the article by imagining Superman's parents giving him a little talk. "So, Superman, we see you're still flying around like a maniac. Why haven't you settled down?" He then goes on to discuss the dating ritual. "I'm 36 years old. I'm a single guy. I date. I think I enjoy it. For me, nothing caps off a week like four hours of solid tension."

In one way at least, Seinfeld is clearly an average guy; he finds women to be strange, alien beings. Men and women think differently, he asserts in the article. While men love women as a group but find it hard to like them individually, women despise the race of men but like them as individuals. The minds of men and women rarely run on the same course. While Seinfeld on a date is admiring the woman's hair, she is thinking, "I can't believe the size of the piece of bread he just put in his mouth." The article ends with a mini-dissertation on the difficulties of the first kiss. Like his act, the article is rather chaste.

If Seinfeld hoped that it would satisfy the press, he was doomed to be disappointed. As his star rose so did the fascination in his love life. Pretty soon he'd be making it into the gossip columns and tabloid papers.

In the late eighties, Seinfeld lived in a split-level, two-bedroom condominium in West Hollywood that was notably bare of furnishings except for an enormous L-shaped sectional sofa. What *was* there was black or gray and perfectly in its place. Jay Leno described it as a "hospital room for stereos." But the sparseness matched Seinfeld's perfectionism and his obsession with cleanliness.

The same sparseness characterized his New York apartment on the Upper West Side. Seinfeld had a stunning fifteenth-floor view of Central Park. Although he had to spend most of his time on the West Coast, he still considered New York his home and pined for it when he was away. "For me," he told the *Boston Globe*, "L.A. is just a business trip. Ten years in the office, and I'm still a New Yorker." When Seinfeld did get back to his Manhattan apartment, he immediately adjusted the time on the clocks. The leather chairs and sofas were sleek, the mantle was bare but for two toy Porsches, and the messiest thing about the place might be a single magazine on the coffee table. The bedroom was painted a deep blue. Seinfeld liked to compare it to "Superman's Arctic lair." And he didn't like it to be defiled by the normal bodily functions of other people. He told *Rolling Stone*, "A friend was recently using my bathroom for No. 2, and I objected. I said, 'Do you have to do that in here?' He said, 'It's a toilet.' I said, 'Nevertheless.'"

Once Seinfeld called his apartment "monklike" and confided to the *Ladies Home Journal* that he liked going to a friend's place which would inevitably be messier and more lived-in and say to himself, "'See, this is a life.' You see the life. If you come to my house you don't see any life." But at the same time Seinfeld wished his own surroundings to stay as they were. The writer Alan Richman speculated in *GQ* that this obsession for order and organization comes from a fear "that life is about to spin out of control." But Seinfeld insists that the media has made too much of his neatness, as if they were "trying to find this raging semi-psycho inside of me."

Performing some 300 times a year, Seinfeld's income was now in the millions. But his austere sensibility meant that he had little interest in leading an extravagant Hollywood lifestyle. Seinfeld had only two weaknesses — for expensive watches and Porsches. When he could afford his first $50,000 Porsche, Seinfeld hesitated even though he had wanted one since he was a kid. "Porsches had that swinging-orthodontist image," he said sheepishly to *New York*. But once the barrier was broken, Seinfeld found it easier to buy a second Porsche. To those who know him the cars (one a four-wheel-drive Carrera) seemed the most important thing in the world to him, and he maintained them meticulously. Later his actor cohorts Jason Alexander and Michael Richards couldn't resist throwing leaves on the hood of one of them when they saw it parked in the studio lot. But *clean* leaves only — they knew to take the joke only so far.

Seinfeld the kid found such a delight in his Porsches that he began to collect them the way real kids collect miniature cars. Soon he had a third and then a fourth Porsche, one a vintage 1958 model. He became known for double-parking one with the lights flashing as he dashed into the Improv or some other Los Angeles club to do a quick ten minutes of new material. In spring 1993, during a rare vacation, he planned to visit the Porsche factory in Stuttgart, Germany. What could be a better holiday souvenir than a new car chosen right at the plant?

It was after his brush with Scientology that Seinfeld discovered Zen. A significant sect of Japanese Buddhism, Zen became known in the United States when the American Beat poets became attracted to it in the 1950s. Zen means "meditation," a method of contemplation which it uses to bring enlightenment to its adherents, who try to infuse their daily

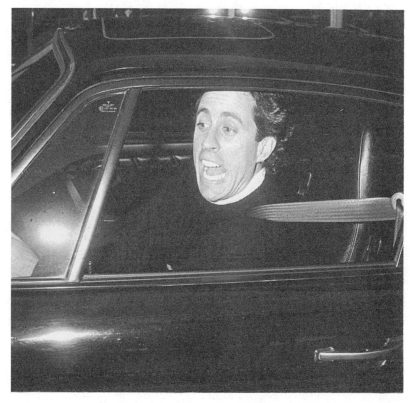

Jerry leaving NBC's Winter Press Tour,
January 14, 1993 — in his Porsche.

lives with a spiritual feeling. Zen fosters a tranquil mental state, lack of fear, and spontaneity — all traits that can be seen in Seinfeld. People attracted to Zen often have a need for calm and a desire for emotional control, or else already have the kind of even and unemotional temper that is naturally suited for it. Seinfeld himself claims to be the latter, without high up or down mood swings — a person who simply doesn't worry about the future.

For twenty years now Seinfeld has been studying Zen, practising yoga, and meditating. Meditation encourages detachment from the external world, even from a sense of joy, until ultimately a person exists in a state of pure equanimity. Perhaps it is Zen, or Seinfeld's natural temperament, that creates that feeling of emotional detachment in his work. But Seinfeld plays down its exoticism, perhaps so as not to make himself look like just another Hollywood flake. He insisted to *People*, "Zen is just looking at something from a different perspective, and that's what comedy is."

If the mind is a temple, then so is the body. Zen, as well as Seinfeld's own ascetic taste, have made him treat his body with respect. His scrupulous approach to cleanliness may have inspired this bit from a monologue on *Seinfeld*: "The human body is a lot of maintenance. It's a lot of showering, a lot of shaving, a lot of cleaning, a lot of checking. If your body was a car you wouldn't buy it. It's too much upkeep." Seinfeld eats health food, drinks mineral water at comedy club bars, and is a fanatical tooth flosser. He's known to floss his teeth just before going onstage.

Likewise, his clothes are always pressed and fresh. His everyday attire is so constant that it has become part of his public identity: jeans, sport shirt, white socks, and most noticeable of all, white Nike running shoes. He owns dozens of pairs of Nikes, all lined up in his closets, and when one gets scuffed he gives the pair away to charity. "The worst thing you can do to

Jerry in his Nike's.

Seinfeld is to step on his white sneakers," Jay Leno snickered to the *Boston Globe*. Once a reporter for *Entertainment Weekly* asked Seinfeld why he insisted on wearing Nikes. Seinfeld answered, "If someone says, 'Hey, do you want to play a game of touch football in the street?' I don't have to go home and change."

No doubt wearing sneakers is connected to Seinfeld's sense of himself as the boy who never grew up. And like most men who remember their youth, he's a sports lover. On his rare leisure time he likes to catch a Mets game at Shea Stadium, play tennis, or ride his bike. When a championship boxing match is shown on pay-TV, Seinfeld and his comedian friends gather around his television to watch and eat pizza. Some good material has come from sports, like his remark on the Olympic luge event, "The only sport where people could be competing against their will and you wouldn't know it."

Now that Seinfeld doesn't have to worry about money, he can go through life with even less aggravation, maintaining the calm he so needs. Once he became wealthy, he simply stopped thinking about money. Seinfeld once made fun of Jay Leno for trying to save a hundred dollars on a VCR. Why bother when Leno is a millionaire? Seinfeld asserted that if a hundred dollars was lying on the next table he wouldn't bother reaching over to pick it up. The flip-side of this lack of concern is a natural generosity, which can manifest itself in unusual ways. Jason Alexander, who would play George on *Seinfeld*, found him to be generous about sharing the good lines in a script. (And there's nothing harder for a comic than to give up laughs.) "He's always on an even keel," Alexander told *People*. "Jerry reminds me — in a very good sense — of a good Jewish boy. Well brought-up, polite, intelligent."

5

NBC Comes Calling

Situation comedy is a genre as old as television itself. Its origins go back even farther, to the pre-television radio shows whose approach to humor was in turn adapted from vaudeville theatre. From the beginning it was a broadly based comedy with a wide appeal and no great intellectual demands. Over the years the sitcom has evolved to the point where, over and over again, the form seems to have exhausted all possibilities. Then a new show will come along — *All in the Family, The Mary Tyler Moore Show, Cheers* — to give it a new life.

Sitcoms are usually set in a home, whether it be Ralph Kramden's spartan apartment in *The Honeymooners* or the Huxtable's house of bourgeois comfort and good taste in *The Cosby Show*. Sometimes the setting is a workplace, such as the police station in *Barney Miller* or the radio station in *WKRP in Cincinnati*, which functions as a kind of surrogate home, with the people who work there acting like a family. Among the cast there's also usually an outsider to help stir up trouble, whether it be the neighborhood busybody or the building superintendent. Usually these people drive one another crazy, but the audience knows that they really love and care about one another. No matter how vicious the sarcasm, how loud they scream at one another, in the end they kiss and make up.

Despite the formula nature of television shows, no television executive has ever come up with a sure-fire recipe for making a hit. For that reason the networks commission hundreds of pilots (a single trial episode of a new show) and often tests them before audiences, hoping that this or that combination of formula ingredients will strike gold. The network might be attracted to a new idea for a show because of the track record of the creator such as Steven Bochco (*Hill Street Blues*) or Gary Goldberg (*Family Ties*) or Diane English (*Murphy Brown*). But even successful producers have more flops than hits. Norman Lear created *All in the Family* but who can remember his show *The Dumplings*? The network might feel safe with a new show that has a bankable actor, but even the star of *The Mary Tyler Moore Show* has failed at subsequent tries. Sometimes an unusual concept might perk the network's interests. *Alf* starred a sarcastic but loveable alien, although in every other way it was standard sitcom formula. It was a success, but *Harry and the Hendersons*, whose novel attraction was a seven-foot-high Bigfoot, wasn't.

In the last few years, television has tapped the talents of comics in the hope that a strong personality and a natural gift for humor will invigorate even a tired sitcom idea. Some comics, such as Richard Lewis in *Anything But Love*, hold viewers interests for a while, until the comic's limited style begins to grate. Some, like Paul Reiser, have audience appeal but can't perform the miracle of making a lousy script funny, and so move on from one show to another in the hope of getting one that works. Many more fizzle out instantly. The Bill Cosbys and Roseanne Arnolds are rare.

Seinfeld knew the pitfalls of television. He'd already had one bad experience with *Benson* and wasn't looking for another. Unlike some performers, he well knew his limitations; he was a comic who played himself, Jerry Seinfeld, not an actor. Just the idea of acting a love scene or having to show a lot of emotion made him uncomfortable. He was already making more money than he needed. On the other hand, a successful television show would thrust him into the top rank of entertainers. Compared to being a television star, stand-up comedy was a rather specialized field. But the chances of finding a television show that interested him were slim.

Not that people didn't try. In the spring of 1988 Seinfeld received an offer to star in a sitcom that was appealing enough for him to consider for a few weeks. The people behind it had until then worked in film and were highly respected in the industry. Seinfeld took some meetings, but as he thought about it his reservations grew. "Don't you feel bad when you see one of your favorite comics doing some [lousy] show?" he mused to the *Los Angeles Times*. He had a much more sure sense of his power and a greater sense of belief in himself than most performers. "If anything," he said, "I'm trying to use the independence that I have to turn stuff down — not to get stuff." Sure enough, a short time later he turned down the offer. It looked as if Seinfeld was not destined for his own television show. But he hadn't counted on NBC.

In that same year, 1988, when Seinfeld's career was really cooking, Brandon Tartikoff, then head of NBC, approached Seinfeld. Born in New York in 1949, Tartikoff had been the youngest person ever to be named president of an NBC division. He shared much of the credit for the creation of such shows as *Hill Street Blues*, *The Cosby Show*, and *Miami Vice*. (Later Seinfeld would joke about Tartikoff, "I look a lot like him — I'm secretly his illegitimate son.") Would Seinfeld be interested in doing a special for the network? Tartikoff didn't suggest any particular format or idea; he wanted Seinfeld to come up with something himself. A production company called Castle Rock Entertainment was interested in packaging the special. Castle Rock was a major player in both television and films, with a solid reputation and plenty of financial backing.

Seinfeld had already done a stand-up special for HBO (whose potential audience was much smaller than a network) and, besides, taped performances weren't really NBC material. No doubt his interest was peaked by the possibility of creating something new, especially as he had vowed to be in control of any new television attempts.

LARRY DAVID, COMIC FAILURE

One night Seinfeld went to a comedy club in New York to find his friend, Larry David. He told David about NBC's offer and asked if David would like to brainstorm with him.

Larry David was also a comic and the two had known one another for years. The difference was that on stage David was a failure. It wasn't that his material wasn't funny — he was actually something of a legend to other comics, who often came to see him perform. But to say that David didn't have the right temperament for performing was like saying that Genghis Khan would have made a lousy social worker. He was a depressive personality, mistrustful, even hostile towards the audience. Seinfeld told *GQ*, "He'd get so angry and resentful if he'd see someone not listening or someone making a noise, he'd completely fly off the handle." He was known to stomp off stage if he felt the audience did not sufficiently appreciate his efforts.

Tall and long-limbed, David had a rapidly receding hairline and an eagle's beak of a nose. On the surface, he seemed a strange choice to collaborate with the even-tempered and genial Seinfeld. A mass of seething neuroses combined with a gloomy shyness, David saw the worst in everything. He was almost unbelievably insecure and at the same time a fatalist who expected to be miserable and perhaps in some masochistic fashion even wished for it. But Seinfeld admired David's writing. Perhaps he guessed that a combination of his own steadiness and David's instability could be potent. Later, Seinfeld would simply say, "Although Larry and I have very different attitudes towards humor, his stuff just fits me."

David was just past 40. The son of a menswear salesman, he grew up in Sheepshead Bay at the foot of Brooklyn. Later an obnoxious comic in an episode of *Seinfeld* would come from Sheepshead Bay. "We were right on the water," he would say in a heavy Brooklyn accent. "The whole atmosphere stank from fish." As a boy, David used to giggle to himself in synagogue and was devoted to Abbott and Costello. Besides doing stand-up, he had been a performer on the ABC show *Fridays*, a poor imitation of *Saturday Night Live* that survived from 1980 to 1982. After that had come a stint writing for the real *Saturday Night Live*.

The night that Seinfeld sought out David's advice, the two of them headed for the Westway Diner on Ninth Avenue to talk. Along the way, they stopped in at a grocery store and traded some impromptu jokes about other shoppers and the products on the shelf. "This is what the show should be about," David said, meaning the comic banter between them.

David and Seinfeld were definitely on the same track, for Seinfeld was thinking about the same premise that he had used for the skits on his HBO special. At the diner, he said, "The number one question when you're a stand-up comedian is, 'Where do you get your material?'" David responded, "That's what the show should be. How comedians come up with their material." Seinfeld looked at David across the table. "They do this," he said. "They hang out with their friends."

From there the two comics began to expand. Comedians found their routines around them, by observing their own lives and those of the people they knew. Above all they liked

ALAN LEVENSON/ONYX

Jerry and Larry David (on right) going over a script.

to talk, so any special about a comic would have to have conversation at its center. Seinfeld could play the comic and the rest of the cast would be made up of his friends. "The idea was that Jerry was supposed to do a *Tonight Show*," David later remembered for the *Boston Globe*, "and he didn't have any new material, so we were going to see how he got the material. And at the end of the special, we'd see him doing the material on television."

The idea was not only original, but it played to Seinfeld's strengths. He would be able to perform stand-up on the special, which was his real talent and love. What's more, he and David decided that Seinfeld should play himself, Jerry Seinfeld, rather than some fictional character. There was already a precedent for it in the recent *It's Garry Shandling's Show*. A major difference would be that unlike Shandling (a talented comic who had yet to find success on a network show), Seinfeld wouldn't break the illusion of reality by talking to the audience. That the idea was a mixing of an old form with a new was shown later when NBC advertised the show as "Part Sit-Com! Part Stand-Up!"

Almost everything was unusual about the origin of the special. For one thing, it wasn't a corporate product, or even the idea of a veteran television producer, but the brainchild of two comics who had little experience in creating a television show. As Seinfeld said, the special was a "two-man canoe." Any other way and Seinfeld would have turned his back on NBC and returned happily to the stage. In truth, neither he nor David really expected NBC to bite — their idea was simply too different. As Seinfeld told *Us*, "Every step of the way we were waiting for somebody to come in and say, 'You can't do this on network TV.'" To their surprise, NBC didn't merely like the idea; the network asked Seinfeld and David to use it for the pilot of a new series.

Seinfeld hadn't been wary of doing a television show only because of the poor quality of so much programming. A show would take him away from doing his own routines. But this project was different. "The only reason I would consider committing to it is that I'd be doing stand-up on the show," he announced to *Playboy*. Added to that was the fact that he and David would receive the coveted "Created by" credit. Those credits that roll at the beginning and ending of shows do more than stroke people's egos; they translate into money. As creators, Seinfeld and David would receive a royalty every time an episode was ever broadcast. (David also had credit as executive producer, and Seinfeld as producer.) Now he and David needed to develop the idea into a fuller situation that would generate future episodes should the show get picked up.

What Seinfeld brought to the show was first and foremost himself. The TV Jerry (as his character came to be called on the set) would be a fictional version of the real Seinfeld — cool, wry, funny, single but dating, a New Yorker living on the Upper West Side. Seinfeld had his previous stand-up material to draw on for the monologues in which he would appear before a club audience (actually a set) delivering jokes based on what was happening during the episode. Although it would appear to viewers as if he was making jokes out of each episode's story, in fact the stories would at first largely be written to fit the monologues. (Actually, a precedent existed for this use of stand-up material. Bill Cosby sometimes incorporated bits from his old act in *The Cosby Show*, weaving them into the script rather than presenting them as routines.)

What David brought to the show was most of the rest. His was the vision that would set the tone and atmosphere: cranky, pessimistic, even dark. It was because of his sensibility that the characters would be (in the words of writer Alan Richman in

GQ) "urban rejectees, the kind of people who could suffer anywhere." None of them would be able to sustain a permanent relationship; instead, they would be almost unhealthily dependent on one another. It wouldn't even be clear that the friends really *liked* one another. The show would have a tart, witty, edgy New York feel. And a vaguely Jewish feel as well, although that would never be made obvious.

Most important of all, David insisted, the show would be about — well — nothing. By nothing, he meant that the plot of each episode would not really matter. More important were the small daily activities that make up people's days, the tiny frustrations, the mistakes and absurdities. Most of life — at least in David's view — is in fact mundane, annoying, and even boring, like losing your car in a parking lot, or not being able to decide whether to take an apartment, or having to talk to old friends you no longer have anything in common with — all moments from future episodes. David wanted to find what was funny in those situations.

"We want the show to be about the problems no one is trained to handle," David explained to the *Washington Post*. "All this education and conversation and parental guidance that you've had in your life does not prepare you for a huge number of things that come up. I think what goes on in people's lives is that most of their mind, most of the day, is occupied with tiny struggles. That's what people's lives are about." He told the *New York Times*, "A sitcom idea, well, you know exactly where it's going to go. But we wanted to do a show where, well, you don't *care* where it goes. At all. As long as it doesn't go where you think it's going to go. Most sitcoms set up the situation and plug in one-liners. We try . . . to make the situation itself funny." Or as Lisa Schwarzbaum would put it in *Entertainment Weekly*, it would be about "the little adjustments of daily urban life that no network in its right mind would turn into a sitcom."

59

David's conception of the show was, despite its intention as a comedy, deliberately dark. He later described it to Elaine Pope, a writer who came on staff, as being about the "horror and chaos of being single in New York." After it had been running for a time, David would insist on his bleak vision to those who preferred to think it was just funny. "A lot of people don't understand that *Seinfeld* is a dark show. If you examine the premises, terrible things happen to people. They lose jobs; somebody breaks up with a stroke victim; somebody's told they need a nose job. That's my sensibility."

Not surprisingly, David insisted that the show carry no life-affirming messages the way most sitcoms did. No little moment of understanding and sympathy, of reconciliation and healing. No lesson in sharing, or tolerance, or anything else. David put it succinctly in words that became the show's motto: "No learning. No hugging."

6

With Friends Like George and Kramer, Who Needs Enemies?

"The concept grew out of not wanting to do a sitcom to begin with," Seinfeld said to the *Boston Globe*. "This to me is as close as I could get to doing 30 funny minutes a week on a TV show without doing a sitcom."

In fact, the show as it developed did share some classic situation comedy elements. Jerry's friends would make up a kind of nuclear family. There would be the best friend who was a loser, the girl (in this case, the ex-girl), and the loony next-door neighbor. Most scenes would take place in Jerry's apartment which would become a substitute home for all the characters. The show would even have a laugh-track, provided by the live audience during taping.

But much more important than the similarities were the differences. And those differences could be seen foremost of all in the characters. Initially the show was intended to be something of a showcase for Seinfeld's act, but as the series developed the other characters won an equal share in the action and, among viewers, a large following.

Since Seinfeld was going to play himself, why not base one of the friends on Larry David? And so George Costanza was born. Despite his Mediterranean name, George was imagined as another thoroughly Jewish New Yorker. (In the show, this question would be resolved by giving George a Jewish mother.) He was made into an extreme version of Larry David — angst-ridden, insecure, stingy, and explosive. In the first episodes he has a job in real estate finding tenants for apartments, but soon he is out of work and unable to hold a job. An article in *TV Guide* would debate whether he was a "schmo," a "schmuck," or a "schlemiel." While all are a form of loser, a schmuck is also a son-of-a-bitch, while a schmo is unlucky and hapless, and a schlemiel is a pitiful social misfit.

George himself insists that he is not a loser. He does, however, realize that his personal problems go beyond the ordinary. "Divorce is very difficult, especially on the kid," he says in one episode. "Of course I'm the result of my parents having stayed together, so you never know." His visits to a therapist (paid for by his mother) usually end with him storming out in fury. "George is the sickest part of me," David said. "A sick part of my personality — but only one side. Most of the time, I'm too morose to get as excited as George does."

George is the sort of guy who goes to his friend Jerry's apartment to watch a video even when Jerry isn't there because it makes him feel as if he's not just doing nothing at home. Whose name — Costanza — was turned into "Can't-Stand-Ya" by the kids in school and who suffered the indignity of an atomic wedgie in gym class. Who can't make a relationship with a woman last or present himself honestly. ("You've got to put on a show, you've got to put on a big show, you always have to be on. Otherwise why would they like me? They'd go for a better looking guy with more money.") Who has a low panic threshold and a tendency to lie during moments of crisis. (When lying he often uses the fake-word "vandalay," a dead giveaway.) He is the sort of guy who imagines what pseudonym he would use if he ever starred in a porno film (Buck Naked) and wonders what they did for toilet paper during the Civil War.

"Once in my life, I'd like the upper hand," George rages in one episode. "I have no hand. How do I get the hand?"

Television critics would have a field day trying to analyze George. Why not, when "Every word out of George's mouth is raw material for Freudian analysis," according to Francis Davis in the *Atlantic*. Davis believed that George's immaturity was revealed by the fact that his favorite author was the sports writer Mike Lupica. Davis also noted that there had been many losers on television, but that actor Jason Alexander "transcends this stereotype by zeroing in on George's deviousness, his raging libido, and his volatile combination of arrogance and low self-esteem. . . . In his own way George is as vain as he is needy." *New York Newsday* would simply call him "the most fully realized schlemiel in the history of television."

As time went on, George would become an ever more important character. His weaknesses made him easier for some male viewers to relate to than the obviously successful Jerry. In one episode George moans about his own future: "I'll spend the rest of my life living alone. I'll sit in my disgusting little apartment, watching basketball games, eating take-out, walking around with no underwear cause I'm too lazy to do a laundry." Strangely enough, women viewers seemed to like George too, despite his chronic inability to tell women the truth or to want them to be anything other than perfect, despite his own multiple imperfections. Those women viewers might be surprised to hear why George has been on so many disastrous dates. Jason Alexander admitted to *Rolling Stone*, "For the first three seasons, Jerry was very uncomfortable being an actor. He didn't want to do anything he didn't feel comfortable doing, like getting angry or having a romantic scene. At that point they didn't feel Kramer could be a secret weapon to women. So the only guy left was me."

Early in the show, the writers would try to make George a little tougher, someone who not only suffered the world's abuse but could dish it out as well. But audiences reacted negatively, preferring George to be a decent guy at heart, and in a rare instance of caring about other people's opinions, the creators pulled back. As the show progressed viewers would discover his difficult relationship with his father and his pathetic self-image. They would also find out how he and Jerry became friends when during a high-school gym class George slipped from a rope and fell on Jerry's head. Seinfeld would tell *New York*, "My relationship with George is the glue of the show. Our conversation is basically the conversation between me and Larry. Two idiots trying to figure out the world." Seinfeld would often find himself playing the incredulous straight-man to George's ridiculous and self-destructive behavior.

The character of George would be as much a creation of the actor who played him as he was Larry David's dark twin. It is a well-known truism in the business that the success of any show is heavily dependent on casting. It isn't enough to get a competent actor to play a role; the choice of actors has to be inspired, so that actor and role seem to the audience to have been destined for one another. When David and Seinfeld saw the audition tape sent in by Jason Alexander, they knew that he *was* George after about ten seconds of viewing. Alexander was the first actor cast after Seinfeld himself and the only one without experience in stand-up or comedy writing. Instead, Alexander was a consummate actor and singer who had won a Tony Award as well as Drama Desk and Outer Critics' Circle Awards for his recent performance in *Jerome Robbins' Broadway*.

Born Jay Greenspan, Alexander adopted his father's first name as his own last for a more impressive sound. While he had appeared in such films as *Brighton Beach Memoirs*, *Mosquito Coast*, and *Pretty Woman*, audiences didn't recognize him. Not yet 30, he was a short, stocky man with a bullet-shaped head and a receding forehead who, as George, squinted uneasily through glasses, wore unflattering plaid shirts and running shoes with the laces untied. George would alternate between couch-potato lethargy and a manic energy. When upset or vulnerable his voice would rise to a shout and his hands would punch the air with desperately ineffective violence.

The real-life Alexander is actually quite handsome and nothing like George. Having grown up in New Jersey, he found George's Nu Yawk accent a short stretch. He was married to actress and writer Daena Title, and the two would have their first child, a son named Gabriel whose life was begun in vitro, after the start of the show. Nor was Alexander much like his co-star Seinfeld. "Jerry, God bless him, with his Porsches," Alexander, who was still driving a 1988 Toyota, laughed to *Rolling Stone*. "I would never spend money on an automobile! It means nothing to me." He did, however, buy a new house in Los Angeles after the show became a hit.

Alexander told the *New York Times* about George, "I envy that he states his opinions so firmly. George is not an equivocator. I can be. He may do an about-face, but it's as thorough as his first attempt." He speculated that "What makes him appealing is that he has a strong female side. Lots of his anxieties are feminine: How do I look? What impression do I make? Am I prepared?" Perhaps what makes George so appealing, though — what softens Larry David's darkness — is that Alexander plays him.

A LITTLE PROBLEM WITH GRAVITY

The only real disagreement that Seinfeld and David had over the conception of the show centered on the last of the three-some of bachelor friends who would make up the show's original core cast. (Elaine was yet to come.) His name in the pilot was Hoffman and he too was based on a real person — a man named Kramer who lived across the hall from David's apartment in New York.

With thinning hair and a rather pleasant face, the real Kramer is not the sort to stand out in a crowd. A former comic, he is a man with no discernible means of income and who prefers the description "entrepreneur" for his various mysterious enterprises. He has a knack for getting things free or cheap, and his friend Larry David was a soft touch. David let Kramer wander in and out of his apartment at will — the same apartment in which he and Seinfeld wrote the show's first five scripts. Kramer had often talked about strange incidents in his own life and David eagerly used them as source material for *Seinfeld* as well as some of their mutual escapades. For example, the episode in which George orders a hair-restoring tonic from China and Kramer videotapes George's head to mark the progress is based on the real Kramer performing the same favor for David.

Rumor has it that the show paid Kramer a token amount for the use of his personality and his real name, which was used after the pilot. While Seinfeld thought a more broadly comic character would work best, David wanted Kramer to be played more realistically. In the end, the character landed somewhere in between.

Hearing of the part from Larry David with whom he had worked on the show *Fridays*, Michael Richards naturally wanted to audition. To prove just what a surprising actor he could be, Richards delivered his lines before the NBC executives while standing on his head. Then he righted himself and promptly tripped over a chair. But Richards didn't need to bother; Seinfeld knew Richards' work as a stand-up and when he heard that Richards was available simply made up his mind. Having other actors read for the part was a mere formality.

In fact, Seinfeld was responsible for Michael Richards' first appearance on *The Tonight Show*. In 1989, when Seinfeld and David were developing the series, Jay Leno called Seinfeld on the telephone. Leno was guest-hosting for Johnny Carson and needed a comic to play the role of Dick Williams, fitness instructor to the stars, for a *Tonight Show* skit. Did Seinfeld know anybody? "What about Michael Richards?" Seinfeld suggested. "Yeah," Leno agreed, "Michael could do it." Richards milked his *Tonight Show* debut for all it was worth, going so far as to wrestle with an out-of-control rowing machine. Watching the show on television, Seinfeld and David were sold.

Seinfeld considered Richards to be a physical comedian on the same level as Buster Keaton, and there are some resemblances — the looming height (Richards is six feet two), the strutting walk, the long and drooping face. Richards' amazing mobility would nicely contrast with Seinfeld's stiffer acting. Seinfeld has said that Richards "can break one second down into a hundred distinct parts."

Richards' father died when he was two and his mother, a librarian, raised him in Van Nuys, California — making him the only cast member not from New York. As a kid he loved Red Skelton and Lucille Ball and won laughs by crashing his bike or walking backwards into class or pretending to have a seizure in a store. "The true awakening was in 9th grade, when I took a drama class at school," he recalled for *Starweek*. "Suddenly I had a purpose in life and it filled me with happiness. I didn't even like school; I went there only because of my friends. Fortunately, my mother didn't care about my terrible grades. 'Well, I guess you're not going to Princeton,' was her only comment after looking at one failing report card."

At Thousand Oaks High School in Ventura, Richards was voted "Most Humorous" in his senior year. At college in the sixties he began working up an improvisational act with Ed

Begley, Jr. who remembers every other theater student doing Richards imitations. But then the army drafted him and sent him to Germany. A civilian again in the early seventies, he enrolled in the California Institute of the Arts as a theater student and then Evergreen State College in Olympia, Washington. After college Richards joined the San Diego Repertory Theatre. He married a woman who was a family therapist in 1974 and the couple had a daughter. In 1979, in addition to regular acting and some less glamorous jobs such as driving a school bus, he began doing stand-up comedy. Considering himself a cross between Robin Williams and Andy Kaufman, he worked fast, one gag flying after another along with a host of voices. Among his influences were the French comedian Jacques Tati (who never spoke) and Imogene Coca. But Richards always considered himself an actor first and stand-up as a means to an end.

Richards' first real break came when Billy Crystal gave him a role in a special he was making for HBO. That led to *Fridays* and a series of guest roles on *Hill Street Blues*, *Cheers*, and other shows, as well as some minor parts in a few forgettable films such as *Problem Child*. A 1987 syndicated sitcom that he starred in called *Marblehead Manor* died a quick death.

In real life, Richards is thoughtful, introspective, and soft-spoken. With an interest in things spiritual, he like Seinfeld has studied Eastern religions and, unlike Seinfeld, wears a crystal around his neck (as does Kramer). He's the sort of actor who needs to understand his character's motivation and history, and for some time he had trouble getting the character of Kramer right. Part of the reason was probably the mixed messages coming from Seinfeld and David, and part was because he was conceived of — despite his origin in the real Kramer — as something of a cartoon. Richards found that if he played him too broadly he clashed with the other actors' more naturalistic styles. The man who considered himself "an

BONNIE SCHIFFMAN/ONYX

eccentricity specialist" had to find a way to make Richards both more eccentric and more precise. He did this by using a kind of Method-acting approach that gave depth to Kramer's zaniness. For example, believing that Kramer — whose source of income is one of the show's continuing mysteries — was the sort of person to shop at flea markets to save money, he started scouring real markets for 1950s shirts. Kramer also owned a lucky polyester sports coat that he believed made him score with women. (Among Kramer's known sources of income are playing the racetrack and devising such invaluable inventions as a tie dispenser.)

In one episode Kramer was supposed to go into hysterics every time he heard the voice of Mary Hart, host of *Entertainment Tonight*. Richards balked at the idea until he found out that there really was such a case, giving him the psychological background he needed. "I work very hard to make this character three-dimensional," he assured *Rolling Stone*.

As for Kramer's elevated hairstyle, Richards had a more mundane explanation for *TV Guide*. "I ran into a bad barber and got a bad haircut." The barber had cut it too short in front, so Richards tried to pull it up and it grew from there. Each season it seemed to inch a little higher. In one episode he lit it on fire with a cigar. Now when he is in public women often want to touch it. "It's electric, it just goes *whoooom!*" he said to *Rolling Stone*. "It just took its own shape. It's fascinating."

Some critics have compared Kramer to the character of Reverend Jim that Christopher Loyd played on *Taxi*, but Richards strongly disagrees. Jim was a drugged-out zombie, and if anything Kramer has a brain that works *too* hard. Both actors, though, employed a kind of energized tremble, Jim because of constant drug withdrawal, Kramer because of an over-supply of kinetic energy.

Much of what makes Kramer Kramer can't be written into the script. As Francis Davis wrote in the *Atlantic*, the man has "problems with gravity." He doesn't merely enter Jerry's apartment, he bursts through the door and skids into the room, rotating on his heel in Chaplin style. "Michael's entrances are completely improvised," Seinfeld has said. "We all stand very clear of the door right before he comes in because you never know what kind of vehicle he might be in." Richards' explanation (on NBC's *Dateline*) shows an actor who can make a virtue out of a necessity. "I came up with this kind of entrance because I had to fit myself into the scene. I *really* gotta come in." Kramer's responses to surprising news are like little benign explosions. He's a master of the double-take or the verbal exclamation, "Whoa!" and "Whoopie!" being his favorites. He might spin 360 degrees or slap himself on the forehead so hard his head fires backwards.

The difference between Kramer and George is not that Kramer has any greater natural attributes, but only that he *thinks* he has. George enviously remarks that Kramer makes money without working and has sex without dating — a true fantasy life. That Kramer can get away with it is due to his ridiculous self-confidence, as overblown in its way as is George's self-hatred. He thinks it's only right that women should desire him, and so he speaks to them with lounge-lizard smoothness (he can make the word "dust-buster" sound salacious) or boasts that he likes to have sex with the woman on top so that she can do "all the work." He manages to seduce a woman who Jerry went out with three times without even getting a goodnight kiss — simply because of his bravado. At a baseball camp where adults get to mingle with old-time players he causes a bench-clearing brawl and punches Mickey Mantle in the mouth because he believes that he's just as good a player as the professionals. Francis Davis called him a "hipster doofus," a description that the show's creators seem to have liked so much they used it in an episode. Kramer is plagued by no doubts about the quality of his genius. When in one episode Calvin Klein makes him into an underwear model, Kramer has no shyness about exhibiting his body in all its glory. It hardly matters that, trying to lean casually against a curved wall, he goes sprawling to the ground.

Like the real person who lived across from Larry David, Kramer has virtually free access to Jerry's apartment. He certainly takes advantage of it, usually heading straight for Jerry's Double Crunch cereal. The first line that Kramer ever said on bursting through the door was, "You got any meat?"

THE PILOT: THANKS BUT NO THANKS

Much of this character development came later. At first, both George and Kramer were fairly restrained versions of their later selves. Seinfeld and David together wrote the pilot, tailoring the material to some of Seinfeld's already existing material. Because Seinfeld had a good bit on laundromats to use in a monologue, they set one of the scenes in a laundromat. Another bit on dogs prompted them to give Kramer a dog, never to be seen again.

The pilot aired on July 5, 1989, and was titled *The Seinfeld Chronicles*. Jerry is performing at a comedy club out of town when he meets an attractive young woman. Hearing that she's going to visit New York, Jerry invites her to stay at his apartment. But shortly after she arrives he's appalled to discover that the woman is engaged. Besides Jerry, George, Kramer, there was a waitress character who was wiser than the guys, played by Lee Garlington.

As *Variety* noted, the pilot was deliberately low key, its humor remarkably understated considering the exaggerated laughs that most sitcoms try for. While the influential paper praised the pilot as promising, it also considered the show a "watered-down" version of Garry Shandling's show, seeing the superficial similarities rather than the differences.

Pilots for new shows are not asked for by networks merely on a whim. They cost about a million dollars to make and the network has to pick up most of the production costs. Once made, they aren't just put onto the air while everyone keeps his fingers crossed. They are heavily tested in private showings before audiences who rate everything from the story to the likability of the characters. In the spring, the network executives combine the research material with their own instincts and come up with a fall season. Most concepts never make it to the pilot stage, and only one out of three pilots becomes a series. Only about two of every ten series gets renewed for a second season. As NBC's Brandon Tartikoff told Richard Levenson and William Link in the book *Off Camera*: "If I had to be black and white about it, I'd say that 80 percent of my function is to compete against CBS and ABC to win every time period. The other 20 percent is what I call the Second Agenda, which really started when Grant Tinker walked in the door. This involves what we can do to further the medium, to improve it. It's everything from the Television Academy Hall of Fame to the occasional movie for television that we produce not because it will get a 40 share — we know it won't — but because it deserves to be put on the air. Plus an occasional television series that you know will probably not be successful but whose creative auspices are impeccable enough to take the long shot."

Apparently the NBC executives didn't believe that *The Seinfeld Chronicles* was going to win a big enough audience right away, and not having crystal balls, they didn't have the foresight to see that the show's potential was worth their taking that long shot. And being a sitcom — a less prestigious form than a drama or a special series on "serious" subject — it wasn't worth losing money on just to look good. As Tartikoff said, "The higher the ratings of my shows, the greater the profits

NBC enjoys. That's the crassest way of looking at my job." And so, despite having instigated the pilot in the first place, NBC decided to "pass" on it — television-speak for "thanks but no thanks." Seinfeld seemed to have been resigned to rejection from the beginning. "Success was not in the plan," he later told the *Boston Globe*. "We just figured we'd fail with something that we were proud of. I wanted people to say, 'Gee, it's too bad they took your show off, it was really good.'"

In any case, he always had stand-up to go back to. As for Larry David, it would have just been one in a long line of dismal career moves, confirming for him that life is lousy and then you die.

7

A Second Chance

Seinfeld did not disappear from television screens altogether after the initial rejection of the pilot. He appeared on HBO's *Just for Laughs Festival* in November 1989, and hosted the *Second Annual Comedy Festival* on Showtime, another pay-tv channel. Nothing wrong with those gigs, except that they weren't network.

Not all the NBC executives had the same opinion of *The Seinfeld Chronicles*. Rick Ludwin, in charge of late-night programming, liked it. The demands of late night are different from the higher-stakes, high pressure prime-time period, where shows compete for the largest audience of the day and need to have wide appeal. Late-night programming attracts a younger and hipper audience and the shows can take more chances. There is less money at stake and so the networks don't keep as firm a controlling hand on the shows. David Letterman is a perfect example of the kind of off-centred, risk-taking performer who would never have been given a shot at prime time but who turned out to be a major hit in a late-night slot. (For that very reason, NBC decided to choose Jay Leno over Letterman to take over *The Tonight Show*. Leno, they believed, has greater mass-market appeal.)

Ludwin offered Seinfeld and David a limited run as a 1990 summer replacement series, saving the show from oblivion. The comics had just four time-slots to fill, a modest quartet of episodes to be shown on Thursdays at 9:30 that would allow them to develop the show a little more and prove its worth. In retrospect, they were fortunate to be given this little training exercise; having to create a full season of shows would likely have overwhelmed them. The first change was to shorten the name to *Seinfeld* so as to avoid association with the short-lived ABC series called *The Marshall Chronicles*.

NBC saw one major flaw in the show's conception: all the stars were men. That wasn't really surprising considering that comedy, despite the success of a few women such as Rita Rudner, is still basically a boy's club. As Julia Louis-Dreyfus expressed it to *TV Guide*, NBC said, "Put in a girl, a broad, a woman." Seinfeld and David complied, but they wanted to avoid the usual stock-character — the woman who has a constant love-hate flirtation with the male star à la *Moonlighting* or *Cheers*. To come up with the character of Elaine Benes they drew on yet another real-life source. Several years before, Seinfeld had dated a woman comic named Carol Leifer. After they broke up, the two continued to hang out together. Elaine would be a former girlfriend of Jerry's, a friendship left over from a failed romance where, to quote Jerry from an early episode, "There was a little problem with the physical chemistry." Only in one future episode would they become lovers again, and that would be over by the next week. Seinfeld believed that it was more interesting to have them dating other people rather than each other. As for her effect on his own character, he called her "the ex-girlfriend you can't seem to get past."

Elaine is the sort of woman who, for some self-destructive reason of her own, likes to be the one girl hanging around with the guys. Although in one episode she sighs, "I've got to

get new friends," she never takes her own good advice. Elaine is the only one on the show with a regular job, as a reader in a publishing company called Pendant Publishing. (At one point she gets George a job in her office, which he loses after having sex with a cleaning woman on one of the desks. The sight of her vacuuming turned him on.) In contrast to the males, she has a political side and is rather strident about her causes: non-smoking, animal fur, feminism. In the final episode of the 1992–93 season she files a complaint against the owner of the local coffee shop, believing that he hires only big-busted women. (They turn out to be his daughters.) At other times her opinion is the voice of sanity next to the views of her male buddies — she's what *Toronto Star* critic Rob Salem calls their "reality check." But Elaine has her neuroses as well and wavers about her own desires and needs. She also has her own callous streak. She breaks up with a boyfriend, a man 30 years her senior, who has a stroke on the same day. Because he's paralysed she speaks to him as if he's an infant.

At first the part of Elaine was fairly small. But when Julia Louis-Dreyfus read the script she was knocked out. "Normally I would have hesitated," she admitted to *People*, "because my inclination would have been to get a lead, right? But the writing was truly spectacular — no bull."

Louis-Dreyfus (pronounced "Louie") was under thirty when she received the script. The child of divorced and remarried parents, she was raised harmoniously by her two families, moving between New York City and Washington, D.C. She began acting in the private girls' school she attended and then entered Northwestern University for theater arts. There she met her future husband, Brad Hall, who headed an improvisational group. Louis-Dreyfus joined the group, setting a precedent for the future by being the only female. In 1982 both she and Hall got picked to join the cast of *Saturday Night Live* by the producers who had seen them in a Chicago comedy revue. But Louis-Dreyfus found the atmosphere on the show "extremely political" and her time there a trying experience. "Ultimately I learned that it's not worth it unless you're having a good time," she told *People*. After that came a part in *National Lampoon's Christmas Vacation* and a starring role as a kid-hating stockbroker in *Day by Day*, a sitcom about a daycare center that fizzled.

"She had an intelligence and appeal that was exactly what we were looking for," Seinfeld also told *People*. George Shapiro, Seinfeld's manager along with Howard West (the show's executive producers), noted her warmth and likability. "It's difficult to be in the same room with Julia without hugging her." Elaine Pope, who later came on as the only woman writer on the show, thought that she was the opposite of a prima donna, an unpretentious and cooperative actress. She did, however, note Louis-Dreyfus' obsession with her amazingly full head of hair: "That's a whole separate career to keep it looking good."

Chris Smith of *New York* admired her "Silly Putty face" and her ability to be both funny and appealing. Critics would say that Louis-Dreyfus stole scenes from the other actors. Actually, they would say that each of the stars stole scenes from one another.

QUARTET

In the quartet of shows produced for the summer of 1990, *Seinfeld*'s basic structure — in so far as it has a structure — was worked out. Most scenes took place in Jerry's apartment which, in contrast to the sprawling lofts usually depicted in movies and television shows, looked like a real Manhattan apartment. The other recurring venue was a restaurant, although its design would later change. In the early incarnation it had stand-alone tables rather than booths and looked more like a Denny's or some other chain than the later typical New York coffee shop.

Each episode was introduced and concluded by a monologue, in which Jerry performed in front of a club audience which the viewer could feel a part of. In the early shows there was also a monologue somewhere in the middle. At the beginning, the director Tom Cherones used more medium shots of Jerry and more reaction shots of the laughing audience. Later the audience would be shown in only a cursory way and the camera would move in closer on Jerry, creating a greater feeling of intimacy for the viewer.

Seinfeld always wrote the monologue material himself. At the start he used some bits from his stand-up routines and some of the show's scenes were written, like the pilot, to fit his material. But as more and more shows had to be created and scripts written to deadline, Seinfeld started to play catch up. He began to write the monologues after the scripts were done. Eventually the monologue in the middle of the show would be dropped, in part because Seinfeld worried about being able to produce enough good material on such short notice. But also as the show progressed it needed the monologues less as a kind of glue holding the scenes together. In time the monologues and the regular scenes began to complement each other more evenly.

Seinfeld has speculated about dropping the monologues all together, but that would undoubtedly be a mistake. For one thing, at their best they are as funny and sharply observant as any of Seinfeld's earlier stand-up routines. For another, they give a purpose to the rest of the show that it would otherwise not have. Finally, they indirectly tell us about the character of Jerry on the show.

Seinfeld found it both easy and a little odd to play the character of Jerry. "It's very bizarre," he said to the *Chicago Times*. "I'm a real person, interacting with fictional people. It's kind of like *Roger Rabbit*." Of course, Jerry is not exactly Seinfeld. "I think the difference between the real-life me and the TV Jerry," he analyzed for the *Ladies Home Journal*, "is kind of like Nice 'n Easy hair coloring. It's me, only better. You know, a little wittier and a little more resourceful, a little more likely to get involved in annoying situations." He admitted to the *Boston Globe* that his real life is less interesting than that of his television *doppelgänger*. "The life of a comic is really about sitting around doing nothing much but thinking. Funny things don't happen: they occur to you."

Like Seinfeld, Jerry on the show is finicky, a perfectionist. He is also more of an observer than a player, unlike the friends who surround him. There's something emotionally reticent about Jerry. Seinfeld as actor increases this feeling by a certain stiffness, but somehow the stiffness works. Never one to claim he's a real actor, Seinfeld says that he just does what he can. "Acting is like riding a bicycle," he said to *GQ*. "You may not compete in the Olympics, but you can keep the pedals going." He admits to avoiding having to do anything intimate on the show, such as kiss a woman or show affection. Unlike Michael Richards, he would hardly feel comfortable strutting around in his underwear.

Yet there are no lack of women for TV Jerry in recent episodes. His difficulties with them are of a different order from either George or Kramer. None of the succession of attractive girlfriends and dates has lasted and the reason is not, as Seinfeld has joked, that they like casting the role too much to have anyone stick. Jerry's problems with women are due largely to his own perfectionist nature. In one episode he enjoys great, uninhibited love-making with a woman, but breaks off the relationship because she's an actress without talent who insists that he read lines with her.

Compared to the more extreme characters of George, Kramer, and even Elaine, Jerry is in some ways the least fully

defined. This works in part because he is the observer who comments on all the rest in his monologues, and partly because he is the "hub of the wheel" around which the other characters spin, as Seinfeld has put it. Glenn Esterly of *TV Guide* compares him to the roles that Bob Newhart played on his succession of shows, but comparisons can also be made with Hal Linden in *Barney Miller* or Judd Hirsch in *Taxi*. They are all normal men in the center of craziness.

Despite its unique humor, *Seinfeld* is still part of the American sitcom tradition. As Richard Blum and Richard Lindheim have written in *Primetime: Network Television Programming,* "Writers who create new series proposals play by the rules of the game. Network program heads may give speeches about innovative programming, but they buy just the opposite. Experienced writers have learned that familiar formulas are more salable than new, untested ideas. New program ideas stand the best chance of interesting buyers only if they are reminiscent of other successes. A writer can create intriguing new premises, rich with characters and plots, but the basic format must remain within the context of successful television programming." What Blum and Lindheim write is also true for *Seinfeld* — to a point. The basic situation is not one to confuse most television watchers, and the configuration of characters is reminiscent of other shows. But there is no feeling of formula in *Seinfeld*, of retreading old ideas and stale jokes. The way the humor emerges from small moments, the tone of the show, the playing down of plot significance, the refusal to preach — these and other characteristics give *Seinfeld* its fresh appeal.

WHAT DO YOU TIP A WOOD GUY?

The first episode of the summer run, really the first of the show as the pilot is not considered a real episode, aired on May

31, 1990. Called "The Stakeout," it was written by David and Seinfeld and directed by Tom Cherones, who would go on to direct almost all subsequent episodes. In the main story Jerry decides he can't ask ex-girlfriend Elaine the name of a woman friend of hers that he wants to date. Finally when he does meet up with the woman, Jerry asks, "So, do you date immature men?" "Almost exclusively," she answers. Also in the episode, George plays a mean game of Scrabble with Jerry's mother, played by Liz Sheridan. Jerry's father on the show is played by Phil Bruns, who will later be replaced by another actor.

In another episode, "Male Unbonding," Jerry tries to break up with an old childhood friend who he now can't stand. Asked why he became friends with the guy in the first place, Jerry answers, "I was ten — I would have been friends with Stalin if he had a ping-pong table." In the end Jerry resigns himself to the conclusion that some people remain friends for life no matter what.

The only episode not credited to Seinfeld and David was written by Matt Goldman. But the two creators always had a firm hand on every script whose tone and attitude and style had to reflect David's vision of the show. Seinfeld has said that although he often takes no credit, he does a fair amount of writing of every script. In this one George tries to persuade Jerry to move into a beautiful apartment near Central Park. An unenthusiastic Jerry examines the fireplace. On hearing that you can have wood delivered, he asks, "What do you tip a wood guy?" Jerry finally agrees to take the place, only there's one problem — George has decided that he wants it too. Like the true immature boys they are, the two flip for it. In the end they both give it up to a waitress they meet in the local restaurant. Naturally, both regret it.

Also in the same episode Jerry's apartment is robbed while he's out of town. Noticing that the thief took his answering machine, he moans, "I hate the idea of someone out there

85

returning my calls." (Neither the policeman nor Elaine get the joke.) The event provides the subject for a monologue: "The police come over to your house, they fill out the report, they give you your copy. Now unless they give the crook his copy, I really don't think we're going to crack this case."

The premise of trying to find a decent apartment in New York is simple but has, as Larry David puts it, "comic potential." Like other early episodes, the story line is no more important than the little moments between characters, the cranky dialogue, the asides. The loose structure allows for non-sequiturs, anecdotes, observations. In later episodes, for example, Jerry thinks apropos of nothing about buying a yoyo, Elaine comes out of the bathroom flossing her teeth, George gets into a rage when his jacket zipper catches. These moments are what Larry David means by a show about nothing.

The earliest episodes are more subdued than later ones. The characters of George and Kramer are still only half-formed. George actually dresses neatly, in a blazer and chinos, is well groomed and even a few pounds lighter. Quite a contrast to the later George, as captured in a conversation between him and Jerry in the 1992–93 season finale:

JERRY: Again with the sweatpants.
GEORGE: What? I'm comfortable.
JERRY: You know the message you're sending out to the world with these sweatpants? You're telling the world, "I give up. I can't compete in normal society. I'm miserable so I might as well be comfortable."

The quartet of summer episodes was a partial success with the critics, maybe not a homerun but a hit to second base anyway. John O'Connor of the *New York Times* called it "an ambitious blend of fiction and reality." While he liked the way the monologues played off the other scenes and found Seinfeld "affably amusing," he also found the character of Jerry "irritatingly passive." *Variety* praised the show for going for "insight" rather than the "cheap shot" but also called it too low-key to be a "blockbuster" and wondered whether it had the right stuff to survive. The *Chicago Tribune* also noted its quieter approach: "In stand-up or sit-com, Seinfeld rarely goes for the big bang, but the overall effect is one of cumulative hilarity." *People* gave *Seinfeld* a 'B' rating. Tom Shales in the *Washington Post* focused on Seinfeld's observational style of comedy: "If Margaret Mead had been a laugh riot, she might have been Jerry Seinfeld."

The critics were pretty accurate. The show was good, but not as good as it was going to become. So far the critics had taken more notice than the television viewers, but this time NBC was encouraged by what it saw. Brandon Tartikoff himself gave it the thumbs up — or at least part-way up. *Seinfeld* would not start again in the fall for the 1990–91 season. Instead, it would have to wait its turn for an opening if another show bombed.

8

Taking Notes from Nobody

Whatever fans *Seinfeld* managed to pick up in its first runs had to have an almost superhuman dedication to the show in order not to miss it. Putting a show on the air and taking it off again, shifting its time slot, running too many re-runs during the seasons — these are sure-fire methods for stifling a show's potential for developing an audience. *Seinfeld* suffered from all these programming obstacles but miraculously managed to survive.

After the four summer episodes, the show disappeared for six months. Then Seinfeld and David got the green light to start up again as a mid-season replacement beginning in January 1991. Its time-slot was changed twice and episodes were pre-empted by coverage of the Gulf war. But while its rating numbers weren't high, the demographics were great. The show was drawing young adult males of middle and upper-middle class status. This was the most desired target group of advertisers trying to sell their products for the simple reason that such people had the most disposable income to spend. The size of an audience is not always as important as its make-up. The commercial time on *Seinfeld* sold more easily than any other show except for the hit *Cheers*.

Julia Louis-Dreyfus and Jerry clowning on the set.

Fortunately, Seinfeld and David and the rest of the gang that created the show were still largely being left to their own devices. David's attitude to the network was made obvious on the day that Warren Littlefield, president of NBC Entertainment, first visited the *Seinfeld* set. Littlefield had the power of killing a show he didn't like. NBC and Castle Rock employees nervously crowded into David's office and stood silently as Littlefield told them his ideas for the direction the show should take. Larry David listened and after Littlefield finished said, "Okay. Now get out of my office." Seinfeld was horrified. There was a long pause and then everyone started to laugh. This must be David's weird sense of humor, right?

But David wasn't really trying to be funny. He simply refused to "take notes" from the network, as the practice of network involvement is called. Virtually all producers at least pretended to listen to network advice for fear of being dropped from the schedule. Creative control had long been a contentious issue between those who made the shows and those who put them on the air, and sometimes uneasy compromises were reached. But whenever NBC tried it with David he simply stared them down. For example, NBC thought that Jerry and Elaine should begin their romantic relationship again and make it a continuing part of the show, which is exactly what every other show would have done. But David and Seinfeld didn't find that an interesting idea. "That was a very unusual situation," the writer Elaine Pope said later. "They don't care if you don't get it. Larry David is basically writing for his own amusement. . . . Larry really has carte blanche to do whatever he wants to do. Nobody's interfering with his vision at all."

During the episodes of the 1991 half-season Jerry gets a new suede coat that impresses everyone but Elaine's Hemingway-esque father, suspects that his apartment cleaner is stealing from him, and helps Elaine get an apartment above his own before realizing what it will do to his privacy. George puts on a wedding band to test the theory that women are attracted to married men, loses his real-estate job after trying to poison his boss, and visits a holistic healer. The disasters of dating continues to be a major theme, as Jerry is drawn against his will into a relationship with a woman who George has broken off with. In one of the season's funniest episodes George works up the courage to call a woman on the telephone but gets her answering machine and, losing his cool, leaves her a nasty message. He and Jerry have to try to retrieve the tape from the machine.

But the episode that got the most attention takes place entirely in "real time" as Jerry and company wait in line at a Chinese restaurant, whose haughty host refuses to seat them. Each of the characters is desperate — Elaine for food, Jerry because he can't remember the name of a women he's taking out, and George for the tied-up telephone. The episode is innovative and risk-taking, for the script had to be truly funny to hold the audience's interest. But it is also one of the best examples of how the show embodies Seinfeld's style of recognition humor. We've all waited in restaurant lines, feeling faint and making silly conversation with our friends. The subject is perfect Seinfeld stand-up material; the episode merely dramatizes it by making use of the individual characters.

Future episodes will make use of similar situations (and special sets), with similar hilarious results, but each takes a different approach. In one episode the friends plan to see a movie together, but a chain of small misunderstandings and impulsive decisions means that they never meet up until the very end. Kramer goes to the wrong cinema, George gets in the ticket-holders instead of the ticket-buyers line, while Elaine tries to hold onto four seats with animal aggression. Meanwhile, Jerry is trapped in a cab with a loudmouth comic named Buckles (played in truly annoying fashion by Barry

Diamond) who tries out bad routines (the reactions of famous historical figures to being caught in traffic) and pleads with Jerry to keep his trenchcoat in Jerry's closet because his own is full. Not surprisingly, going to the movies is a ripe subject for Jerry's monologues. He confesses to being one of those people who can never understand the plot and has to whisper questions to his friends: "Why did they kill that guy? Wasn't he with them? Why would they kill him if he was with them?" Perhaps there has never been a show more successful at dramatizing a comic's style.

A DATE WITH THE GALAXY

Much later Jason Alexander would say that "It was critics and journalists who kept us alive" before a large audience caught on. Beginning as a mid-season replacement, *Seinfeld* began — and would continue — to get the kind of reviews that are a network's second-biggest thrill. (The first is high ratings. Positive reviews, alas, don't bring in profits.) Francis Davis in the *Atlantic* called it "the funniest and best written of all current shows. So much in *Seinfeld* is new to TV, beginning with its acknowledgement of the absurdity of the ordinary. . . ." Chris Smith of *New York* crowed, "*Seinfeld* doesn't feel like sitcom television: it feels more like a conversation with your funniest friends." Phil Rosenthal of the *San Francisco Chronicle* named it "one of the funniest, freshest, most intelligent shows. . . ." James Kaplan of *Mademoiselle* joined in: "Let me trumpet it from the housetops: *Seinfeld* is the best show on TV."

But even superheroes have their weaknesses, and not all critics found *Seinfeld* a perfect show. *Time*'s Richard Zoglin wrote in an otherwise positive review published in August 1992, "All that's missing from *Seinfeld* is some human ballast to the frivolity. . . . Seinfeld the character remains curiously weightless and remote." Zoglin complained that the show avoided dealing with the real difficulties between Elaine and Jerry. "A viewer can relate to *Seinfeld* in all the little ways but none of the big ones."

The emotional distance noticed by Zoglin probably didn't bother most viewers who liked the show for being so funny, but it was true. It was one of the traits of Seinfeld the comic and person that carried into the show — a certain dislike of getting too close to the emotions or showing any vulner-ability. When Lawrence Christon criticized Seinfeld in the *Los Angeles Times* he was touching on the same thing. Yet paradoxi-cally this emotional distance is part of what makes Seinfeld the comic he is. It allows him to step outside of himself and observe life around him as if he were an anthropologist study-ing an aboriginal people. And if he seems a little aloof on the show, his coolness is countered by the more extreme temper-atures of the other characters. Perhaps viewers even feel a certain poignancy in Seinfeld's inability to show extremes of emotion. No wonder this man lives alone.

In any case, as every television executive knows, good reviews cannot produce a hit show. They can, however, help a show with marginal ratings. And despite being jerked around the schedule, *Seinfeld* was now getting people talking. That *Seinfeld* just might be the next big thing in television was acknowledged by Seinfeld being chosen to co-host the 43rd annual primetime *Emmy Awards*, along with Dennis Miller and Jamie Lee Curtis. Before the show's live airing on August 25, 1991, Seinfeld tried out his jokes at the L.A. comedy clubs. His own show had kept him so busy that he felt rusty from not getting before an audience enough.

Seinfeld had three nominations, including two for writing — episodes written by Seinfeld and David and by David himself. Tom Cherones was also up for best director. But when the envelopes were opened *Seinfeld* came up with zip; it was shut out by CBS's *Murphy Brown* which was beginning its own wave of popularity. Seinfeld tried to hide his disappointment.

During the broadcast Kirstie Alley came up to the microphone to accept her award for *Cheers*. She thanked her husband "for eight years of giving me the big one." Coming up after her, Seinfeld asked the audience what she meant. "She could have been talking about anything, like a balloon mortgage." Afterwards, Seinfeld said that he had felt like a batter seeing an easy pitch come over the plate. He didn't even know what a balloon payment was — the words just came to him.

But Seinfeld's most memorable joke came when he talked about debating whether he should ask Miss U.S.A. or Miss Universe for a date, both of them being on the show. "I didn't know whether to go for the entire nation or the galaxy."

9

Racing the Fatman

The modest success of *Seinfeld* as a mid-season replacement, combined with the critics' praise, convinced NBC's Warren Littlefield to give it a first full season in 1991–92. *Seinfeld* has "earned its right to be a full-time member" of the schedule, Littlefield told the *Los Angeles Times*.

In order to promote the show in the hope of increasing its audience, NBC put Seinfeld the stand-up comic on the road. With the unwieldy title of *Trident and Certs FreshFruit Presents: The NBC Comedy Tour Featuring Jerry Seinfeld*, the tour took Seinfeld to San Francisco and 18 other cities, ending in mid-July.

NBC must have been pleased with the ratings of the season opener, shown on September 18, which beat its competition. But as the season went on, the show did not maintain quite that standing. Usually it finished second to either *Doogie Howser, MD* on ABC or *Jake and the Fatman* on CBS. A frustrated Seinfeld told *New York*, "It seems that every time we're about to pass *Jake*, the Fatman gets a little fatter and we can't squeeze by." Seinfeld's salary was $40,000 an episode — or $880,000 for the season. Not bad, although hardly in the same league as Ted Danson, who was said to be making half a million a week on *Cheers*.

To the viewer *Seinfeld* seems a thoroughly New York show, from the whining eccentricities and obsessions of the characters, to the bizarre dating rituals, to the constant searches for a better apartment. It's also one of the few shows that makes the city seem like a livable place, rather than a sleazy and crime-infested nightmare. In fact, everything that is really New York about the show — namely the actors (except for Richards) and the writers — is imported. The show is taped on the CBS sound stages of CBS Studio Center in Hollywood and the sets are a constructed fantasy, a parallel New York under theatrical lights and with rows of audience seats in front. Unlike a drama such as *Law and Order* which is set *and* filmed in New York, a situation comedy uses almost all interior scenes. Taping in Hollywood is both cheaper and more convenient.

The show's main setting is Jerry's apartment on West 81st Street on the Upper West Side. Besides being the neighborhood of Seinfeld's real apartment, the Upper West Side is likely where you'd find a Jewish boy made good. Unlike the Waspish and old money Upper East Side, the west is a popular Yuppie neighborhood that has become gentrified only in the last ten years or so. The exterior establishing shot of Jerry's apartment house looks like a classic pre-war New York building, with an awning over the entrance. Actually it's a building in Los Angeles, one of many built in imitation of New York architecture.

David Sackeroff, the original designer on *Seinfeld*, created a fairly tight but workable layout for the apartment. While the living room is the main acting area, the kitchen alcove opens to the audience's right, with a typical New York bar-and-stool arrangement to make most use of space. Directly behind are the doors to the bedroom and the bathroom. The bathroom gets more play than on other shows, where people seem to live without one. On *Seinfeld* people also watch television and

CATHERINE NAGEL, PHOTOGRAPHY

constantly open the refrigerator in search of something to nosh. The set allows for the show's little touches of reality. People worry, they drive each other crazy, and they go to the bathroom.

The "dressing" of the apartment was rather spartan and uninteresting in the earliest episodes. Jerry even had *chrome* shelves. While it shared more of Seinfeld's only taste for austerity, the place wasn't very warm or appealing. Thomas E. Azzari, the set designer who replaced Sackeroff, gave it some texture and a more dishevelled quality. Among the pictures on the fridge is one of Superman. No less than 17 boxes of cereal line a kitchen shelf and the products that can be seen around all have real brand names — another touch of reality. Perhaps the nicest touch is the bicycle hanging on the wall. The apartment has almost the feel of a student's digs and helps to warm up Seinfeld's character. Azzari also made changes in wall color and replaced the kitchen counter.

The second-most used setting, encountered at least once in most shows, is the coffee shop. This time for the exterior shot the producers went to the real New York, more precisely to Tom's Restaurant at 112th and Broadway, just south of Columbia University on the Upper West Side. Usually the exterior is shot so that the word Tom's on the sign can't be seen (thus avoiding the need to pay the real restaurant's owners) and on the show the place is called Monk's. Not that the name is ever spoken (the cast just calls it "the coffee shop"), but it can be glimpsed in reverse on the glass door. Likely the writers came up with a name that looked like Tom's in case a viewer should notice.

The coffee shop is essentially used as a substitute dining room for the friends, a setting for witty conversation, outpourings of George's angst, and occasionally attempts to meet women. The interior is a set built next to the apartment set on the soundstage; it doesn't look anything like the real down-at-heels Tom's. Instead, the set is designed to look like one of the countless clean, nondescript coffee shops that dot Manhattan, each of which has an almost identical menu of breakfast specials and tuna melts. A viewer who's a stickler for accuracy might notice that the interior doesn't match the exterior shot. Tom's has high glass windows on two sides and a corner door, while the interior has only one window and a side door.

Occasionally a script calls for a shot of some well-known New York landmark, or the front of a building where a scene is supposed to take place, or a subway entrance. In these cases, Castle Rock hires a freelance crew in New York to shoot some footage. Those few seconds of Manhattan bustle help to convince the audience to believe that Jerry and friends live in the Big Apple.

Each episode has an art budget of $11,000, not a lot but then sitcoms don't often require many new sets every week. Sometimes the budget goes over the top, like the time a 320-seat section of Yankee Stadium had to be recreated, at a cost of $16,000. Two episodes in 1991–92 were particularly challenging. One, written by Larry Charles, follows the friends on the New York subway. Elaine is on her way to be "best man" at a lesbian wedding. Jerry, going to Coney Island, falls asleep only to awake to the sight of a naked man across from him. Kramer gets chased through a train by muggers after his racetrack winnings. And George meets an alluring woman on a train, whose invitation to join her causes him to skip an important interview. Elaine has a panic attack when her train stalls, Jerry ends up eating hot dogs at Nathans with the naked man, Kramer is rescued by an undercover cop, and George ends up handcuffed to the bed in only his shorts as the woman steals his money and clothes. ("Will I see you again?" he asks her.) The subway-car interiors were built and made to move convincingly by having two grips (workers on the set) hold an end of a pipe attached to each and shake it. Azzari did not recreate a specific subway line, but combined elements of several to create a general New York feel. Because the episode was set in the winter, the actors had to wear heavy coats and scarves even though it was actually a mild day in Los Angeles.

The other difficult episode of the season took place entirely in a mall parking garage. Yet another show set in a single location, it elaborated on a joke that could have been from Seinfeld's act — how you can never find your car at the mall. The show's regular set had to be "struck" or dismantled, a costly and time consuming process, as the entire soundstage was needed. Just as *Seinfeld* is a show that stretches the sitcom form, so the demands of the scripts stretch the abilities of those who work on the technical side, and who must keep within time and budget constraints.

SIX WRITERS IN A STATE OF PANIC

But before any new sets are built, before the cameras roll, comes the script. A season is 22 episodes long and that's a lot of writing, especially when Seinfeld and David wished to maintain firm control of the show. The two comics, along with the writer Larry Charles (who is also the show's supervising producer) managed to keep most of the work for themselves in the early short seasons, but they could hardly keep up with the demands of a full season. For 1991–92, three new regular writers were hired, Peter Mehlman, Elaine Pope, and Tom Leopold, all except Pope (a Canadian) from New York. Even Pope (who later quit to work for the show *Love and War*) shared their "cynical, sarcastic attitude" and "cranky" sensibility, according to Seinfeld in GQ. None of them had ever worked on a sitcom before nor had particularly wanted to, in contrast to the veteran television writers who move from show to show. They weren't even TV watchers.

That lack of experience helped to make their writing fresh, iconoclastic, and free of most television clichés. *Seinfeld* viewers are not subjected to the typical sitcom rhythm of a joke every third line. After a while *Seinfeld* began to receive more unsolicited scripts than any other show, but writers outside the staff rarely understood their kind of comedy. "We don't really know what we're doing," Seinfeld told the *Washington Post*. "I think that's a thing in our favor." As Jason Alexander explained to *New York*, "These guys don't write jokes. They write angst from a character point of view. It's more like people talking." When at the end of the 1991–92 season they did a show with the cast of *Murphy Brown*, the cast and crew of *Seinfeld* were amazed to see what a smooth-running machine that show was. Compared to them, *Seinfeld*'s makers looked like a bunch of kids putting on a show in a Mickey Rooney film.

Seinfeld has acknowledged that the show named after him is largely the creation of Larry David. "Most of the stories are from his life, almost all of it. He just has a tremendous well-spring of ideas. I mean he just fills notebooks with ideas and I try to help him, but Larry is really the designer of the show. There are just some people who literally have funny lives and things happen to them that sound like stories. He has that kind of life." Not surprisingly given his morose nature, David put his source of inspiration in a different light. "My life has been pretty depressing, actually. I feel I am completely devoid of experiences. Other people, they travel, they do things, they have a life. My experiences are so minor. I go for acupuncture or I see something strange on the subway, big deal."

Perhaps what helped to make the show unique was that most of the things that happen on it are based on real life. Elaine Pope confirmed the fact during an interview on *Morningside*, a Canadian Broadcasting Corporation radio show. "Larry wants to do stories that are as much as possible based on things that happened to people on the show. So if some dreadful thing happened to you, he's dying with laughter and that's the show. Pretty well everything that's happened on that show has happened to someone on the staff."

On most days David, Seinfeld, and the other writers had lunch together on the lot. Besides bickering about which restaurant to order from, they batted around episode ideas. The simple test for a good idea or line was whether it broke the other writers up. "The conversations — I can't even begin to tell you," Elaine Pope said on *Morningside*. "They were pretty unbelievable conversations. They mainly centered on food and women and also who thought they had a tumor."

In the early episodes events were always secondary to the incidental moments, the conversation between characters, the clever or dour observations. Over time, though, stronger stories began to emerge, if rather unconventional ones. For example, during one writers' meeting a story line came up involving Jerry witnessing someone sideswipe a parked car. Jerry could follow the perpetrator, only to discover that the driver was a beautiful woman. But what if the victim of the swipe turned out to be another woman Jerry was dating? Then the writers decided that a subplot was also needed. George could be pursued by a married woman wanting to have an affair.

Seinfeld described his image of the writing staff for the *Washington Post*: "a bunch of guys who stand around all day in the hallways, wearing sneakers and talking about sports, and somehow at the end of the week, there's a show." Actually, the truth was a little different. Scripts did not appear by magic — nor necessarily on time. *Seinfeld* was a seat-of-the-pants operation, with the writers often scrambling at the last minute to rewrite scripts, even to write scripts to fill holes in the line-up, especially as the season progressed. It seemed as if David's peculiar temperament required the world to be in a constant state of flux, with disaster looming around the corner, for his creative inspiration to flow. Larry Charles described their method-in-madness for the *Los Angeles Times*: "We don't have a grand scheme. From week to week we just try to do the funniest possible show we can. We are in a complete state of panic virtually week to week in trying to come up with a great show. In that panic-stricken mode, we throw around ideas and we think about stuff."

THE TABLE-READ

The first step in the filming of a script is the table-read, where the actors sit around a table and simply read their parts aloud. Leaning over and listening with anxiety are the writers, NBC and Castle Rock executives, producers George Shapiro and Howard West, and assorted others. It's a terror-ridden moment for the writers as they strain to hear if their lines get laughs. If there isn't much sound in the room beyond the actor's voices everyone starts to lose confidence in the script.

After the read-through, everyone attending enters into a discussion of the script's strengths and weaknesses. The next day is a long one of rehearsal. Despite the anxiety there's an atmosphere of fun on the set and Seinfeld, Alexander, Louis-Dreyfus, and Richards constantly make each other laugh. Sometimes they go a little nutty from so much intense yet monotonous work going over their lines and learning the blocking from the director. So they may start cutting up, ad-libbing jokes, or speaking their parts in British accents. At 4 p.m. a run-through takes place with those always-nervous writers present. Then the writers go away again and rewrite.

The next day the writers hand out a revised script. In the afternoon a full run-through takes place which is supposed to go smoothly. If it does, the actors get the weekend off. Tuesday is the scheduled shooting day. Shortly before 7 p.m.

Seinfeld changes into his costume — Nike running shoes, and a shirt and pair of jeans virtually identical to the ones he has just removed. The taping occurs before an audience and Seinfeld or another of the actors will come out to warm the audience up. Sometimes Jason Alexander even tries his hand at a little stand-up, proving that good actors don't necessarily make good comedians.

The value of taping before an audience has been explained by producer Gary Goldberg in Richard Levenson and William Link's book, *Off Camera*. "Having an audience present is a great advantage. It gives a tremendous amount of energy to the actors, and you get a very strong, and hopefully legitimate, laugh track." But the show that the audience in the studio sees is not exactly the same as the one that will later be broadcast. Sometimes the show will be taped without an audience one or more times; sometimes the episode will be taped before two successive live audiences. Because a new script must be learned every week, actors inevitably blow some lines. The director and editor later take the various tapings and edit them into a seamless whole. Not only do they have a choice of several takes, but since three or four cameras are rolling during each taping, they have the same number of perspectives to choose from. Because of the number of times the actors must play through the episode, taping is not finished until about 11 p.m.

To let off some steam afterwards some of the staff, Seinfeld included, head over to Jerry's Famous Deli, a New York-style restaurant where Hebrew National salamis hang overhead. Sitting in a horseshoe booth they kibbitz, talk about how the taping went, and gossip about other people in the business.

Sometimes Seinfeld will skip the Deli and instead drive in his Porsche over to one of the comedy clubs to try out some monologue material for an upcoming show. John Milward of the *Boston Globe* captured one of these nights in a 1991 article:

"Jerry Seinfeld enters the Improv like he's got a piece of the action. He avoids eye contact with the patrons of the Los Angeles bar and restaurant and strides directly to the celebrated showroom in the rear. He is greeted by the stage manager, who whispers that he can have ten minutes. . . ." Even if he didn't have to go to try out a routine for the show, Seinfeld would go just to do some stand-up. As he said to the *Chicago Tribune*, "You have to do it very intensively to maintain the edge of it. It's like being a fighter pilot; you can't do it on weekends. You have to really do it, or you could get killed."

The very next day the whole cycle starts again, with a table-read of the new script which may have been written in the previous three or four days. One reading that didn't go well in the 1991–92 season was the episode called "The Dog" that Larry David had based on the recent experience of having acquired a golden retriever puppy. In the script Seinfeld meets a man on a plane and ends up having to take care of his dog for a weekend. The second act seemed particularly weak and the people listening around the table radiated uneasiness. Then someone made a helpful suggestion and other ideas started to come. The writers spent that afternoon revising the story line which by dinner had changed substantially — so much that the actor playing the character of Gavin, the man who owns the dog, had to be replaced.

Another problem with the same episode arose when NBC, which vets all scripts, objected to the use of the word "schmuck." Although most people think the word just means something like jerk, in Yiddish it literally means "penis." While television dramas can get away with more risky language, the networks are more conservative with sitcoms. This was one battle that Larry David didn't win; in the end, the word was dropped from the script.

OVERSEXED DOGS, ASTRONAUT PENS, AND FAULTY CONDOMS

Despite its rocky beginning, "The Dog" turned out to be one of the season's best episodes. Gavin Polone, a boring intellectual in the original script, was turned into a drunk. (His name was borrowed from Larry David's agent.) Travelling with his dog Farfel, Gavin gets sick and asks Jerry to take care of the dog for the weekend. But Farfel turns out to be a terror, wrecking the apartment and shredding Jerry's plans for the weekend. At his wits' end, Jerry considers taking the dog to the pound. When Elaine tells him that the pound will put Farfel to death, Jerry replies, "Really? How late are they open?" Elaine herself gets a great line when she threatens Gavin: "You better pick up your dog tonight or he's humped his last leg."

The lovable Farfel is never actually seen on the show, but only heard, his bark provided by an actor specializing in dog imitations. About this odd profession Seinfeld wrote in *GQ*, "No matter how uncomfortable or out-of-place you may sometimes feel in your present occupation, remember, somewhere, men are barking like dogs for a living."

While the Jewish sensibility of the show usually remains as subtext rather than being openly stated, one episode in the season did dare tackle the subject of anti-semitism in a comical way. Remarkably, it succeeded. Members of a neo-Nazi group called Aryan Alliance mistake Jerry and George for two of their leaders. They get trapped in a limousine with some group members on the way to a rally, one of whom is a chilly but beautiful woman. As always, desperate George can't resist even this opportunity. "Did you see the way she looked at me?" he says. Jerry answers incredulously, "She's a Nazi, George. A *Nazi*." George says, "I know . . . she's kind of a cute Nazi." But the highlight occurs when George, afraid that the

Nazis are about to unmask them, begins to rant, "Astroturf? Well, you know who's responsible for that, don't you? The Jews. The Jews hate grass."

Among the shared experiences in the lives of Seinfeld and David is the retirement of their parents to Florida. This isn't all that surprising, given the number of older people who do flock to the south. David must have had a good deal of fun writing an episode in which Jerry and Elaine visit Jerry's parents to attend a dinner in honor of his father as the outgoing president of the condominium association. Played by Barney Martin and Liz Sheridan, Morty and Liz Seinfeld are the sort of people who don't talk. They argue. They raise eyebrows. They sigh. They argue some more. The other relatives speak their minds just as freely. Jerry's aunt says, "We saw you on *The Tonight Show* last week. I thought Johnny was very rude to you. He didn't let you talk." His uncle tells him to get some new material — the bits he used on Carson were already stale.

When Jerry admires a pen belonging to his father's friend Jack (the same kind used by astronauts, it writes upside down), Jack reluctantly gives it to Jerry. Soon word spreads throughout the condominium that Jerry forced the poor man to give up his favorite pen. Feelings get out of control as the condominium association dinner turns into a brawl. "What is going on in this community?" Jerry asks in bewilderment. "What is driving you to this behavior? Is it the humidity? Is it the Muzak? Is it the white shoes?"

Certainly the most famous episode of the season had Jerry meeting the former New York Mets player Keith Hernandez. It was a brilliantly funny exploration of how men worship sports idols. "He wants me to help him move!" Jerry announces after a phone call. But moments after he has second thoughts that allow him to make a Seinfeldesque comment on the tradition of helping friends move. "I said yes, but I don't feel right about it. I mean, I hardly know the guy." Mostly the episode was a satire on Oliver Stone's film *JFK*, with the incident under examination from myriad points of view not an assassination but a spitting incident.

But the season's funniest episode, called "The Fix Up," was written by Elaine Pope and Larry Charles. Elaine Pope explained on *Morningside* how it too was based in reality. "[Larry Charles] and I are old friends and we fixed up a couple of friends. I had a girlfriend named Cynthia and he had a boyfriend, Bob. I made the big mistake of not meeting Bob beforehand. As their relationship deteriorated and became uglier so did ours. He would come in and say, 'Your bitch girlfriend didn't call Bob,' and I would say, 'Why should she call him if she doesn't like him?' It got really ugly until one day we were screaming at each other. Larry David came in and said, 'What's going on?' He said, 'This is hilarious. This is a show.'"

"The Fix Up" opens with a set of parallel scenes. George is complaining to Jerry about not meeting any women, while Elaine is listening to her friend Cynthia (played by Maggie Jakobson) who is complaining equally vehemently about the lack of available males. Cynthia is attractive, intelligent, and a touch bulimic; she likes to throw up after meals. Jerry and Elaine decide to fix their friends up, but not before they themselves have an argument about the relations between the sexes. "You know what your problem is?" Elaine scolds. "Your standards are too high." Jerry answers meanly, "I went out with you." Elaine lobs back, "That's because my standards are too low." What adds a certain sexual *frisson* to the episode is that George and Cynthia are unspoken substitutes for Jerry and Elaine. Bringing them together is like having sex by proxy.

At first George refuses to go on a blind date, calling it "one step away from personal ads. And prostitutes." Then he proceeds to quiz Jerry about Cynthia — does she have cascading hair, is her voice mellifluous? This from a man who wears ugly shirts, squints, is balding, and leaves his shoelaces undone. But these ridiculous demands of George's aren't only funny, they're a sadly accurate reflection of many middle-aged bachelors' minds. "Smarter than me?" he asks suspiciously. "I don't want anyone smarter than me."

Not only do George and Cynthia go on a date, but they have sex the first night. In George's kitchen. "How good could it be?" Cynthia whines to Elaine. "My head was on a hotplate." Disaster seems near when the condom that Kramer gave George turns out to be defective and Cynthia's period is late. But rather than worrying, George shouts with a surge of male pride, "My boys can swim!"

KRAMER GOES HOLLYWOOD

The season finale, written by Larry Charles and aired on May 6, allowed Michael Richards (who usually has to settle for "fourth banana" as he has put it) to really strut his stuff. After Kramer abuses his possession of a set of keys to Jerry's apartment by bringing in a woman and other infractions, Jerry takes them away. Kramer is devastated, for the keys are a symbol of friendship and trust. But he realizes thoughtfully that he himself "broke the covenant of the keys." In an unusual moment of vulnerability, he looks at himself and realizes that using Jerry's place has been away of avoiding his own problems. "I ignored the squalor in my own life because I'm looking at life through Jerry's eyes." This revelation is the catalyst for his decision to head for California and become an actor, having previously caught the acting bug as an extra in a Woody Allen film. (His one line, "These pretzels are making me thirsty," ended up on the cutting-room floor.)

In a very funny scene Kramer tries to convince George that he too has to reevaluate his life. After proving that George has no present or future prospects, Kramer asks whether he has any real reason for getting up in the morning. His self-confidence devastated, George trembles, "I like to get the *Daily News*." But George stays and Kramer leaves on his own. Only his car breaks down and he has to hitchhike to California, encountering various adventures along the way with a biker, a van of crazed hippies, and an alluring female truck driver. The character Newman also appears in the episode. An occasional regular, Newman is played by an actor of immense girth and boyish face named Wayne Knight. A Broadway actor who has appeared in films such as *Jurassic Park*, Knight gets recognized on the street most often for his *Seinfeld* appearances.

The episode comes to a glorious climax when Jerry and Elaine are watching *Murphy Brown* on television, a show on the rival network CBS that stole two Emmy Awards from *Seinfeld* the previous season. Jerry and Elaine can't believe their eyes: Kramer has a role on *Murphy Brown*! He is playing Steven Snell, Murphy's new secretary, and we see him on Jerry's television screen typing like a madman on a computer keyboard. Murphy, heavily pregnant with a child whose father has not been revealed, says, "Steven Snell, I have a very good feeling about you."

Actually, Murphy Brown wasn't the only pregnant woman on the show that episode. So was Julia Louis-Dreyfus — only she didn't have to stick a pillow under her dress. Louis-Dreyfus, who was expecting her first child, was noticeably round. The director, Tom Cherones, tried to obscure the fact by dressing her in oversized clothes and hiding her behind a mound of towels. In Jerry's apartment she sat with a sofa cushion in her lap. During the first episodes of next season, Louis-Dreyfus' part had to be reduced and her schedule arranged to allow her to care for her new baby, Henry. She worked half days and had a nanny on the set to help her.

During the 1991–92 season *Seinfeld*'s ratings steadily climbed.

Word of mouth abut the show began to bring to it more and more viewers. *Seinfeld* became the show that people were talking about over water coolers and at restaurant tables. Those in the know made in-jokes to one another about the fruit drinks Jerry keeps in his fridge (Snapple) and quoted lines such as "Are those the panties your mother laid out for you?" that made them bend over with laughter while leaving non-initiates with puzzled looks on their faces. *Seinfeld* was a cult show that was quickly growing into a popular success.

That imminent popularity was mirrored by praise from the industry. At the 1992 *Emmy Awards* the show received nine nominations, including one for Seinfeld as best actor in a comedy. While *Murphy Brown* again swept a number of awards (thanks in part to Vice-President Dan Quayle who condemned Murphy's celebration of single motherhood), *Seinfeld* picked up its first Emmy. Elaine Pope and Larry Charles took home statuettes for writing "The Fix Up."

All the signs were there. *Seinfeld* was about to become a hit.

That Championship Season

That *Seinfeld* would survive in the ruthless world of television programming, where every Monday network executives and producers rush to check the previous week's ratings, was never a sure thing. Its creators had no previous experience yet insisted on making the show that they wanted. Its first audience was small and no one would have been surprised if the network had considered the show too quirky, too New York, too sophisticated (one episode made a reference to the writer John Cheever's bisexuality), or too much about nothing to appeal to the mass of television viewers. They might have become fed up with Larry David's refusal to accept notes from the NBC brass. Executives at Castle Rock thought over and over again that NBC was about to pull the plug.

But now it looked as if *Seinfeld* was poised to break out. Seinfeld's salary for 1992–93 was upped two-and-a-half times, to $100,000 an episode. Commercial time for the show sold quickly at $200,000 for 30 seconds. During the 1992 summer Olympics, NBC ran an aggressive advertising campaign with commercials called "Seinfeld Olympic Moments." The network was building for a huge fall opening, hoping that the show would jump into the top 20 or even ten.

The problem for NBC was to get those people who had now heard the buzz about *Seinfeld* but who weren't fans to tune into the show. To do so it took the highly unusual step of ordering two new episodes to run during August. Larry Charles wrote a two-parter that follows Kramer in Hollywood in the wake of the previous season's final episode. Jerry and George also head west as Jerry has an appearance to make on *The Tonight Show*. (He flops because a hotel maid throws out the napkin on which he's written a new joke and he can't remember it.) There they discover that Kramer is being sought by the police, who mistakenly believe him to be the "Smog Strangler."

Larry Charles evidently has a liking for writing in cameo appearances and there is a funny bit in the first part where George Wendt from *Cheers* and Corbin Bernsen from *LA Law* (both NBC shows) have encounters with George and then as guests on *The Tonight Show* talk about the nitwit they've just met. But the story-line about the serial killer is a serious mistake, mostly because the parody of crime scenes just aren't funny; they remind viewers too much that young women really do get murdered in this world. One of the show's faults, noted by some critics, is a general insensitivity to women, not to mention minority groups. (The character of Babu, a Pakistani who ends up deported because of Jerry, is a case in point.) The funniest moments in the second part have nothing to do with the story, but show Jerry and George acting like a couple of kids in the hotel room they share, and wanting to sound the siren inside a police car.

The two episodes failed to win the large audience that NBC had hoped for. The first one drew only middling ratings, nine percent lower than the previous season's average, perhaps because August is not a big month for television watching. The audience for *Seinfeld* would grow, but it would still take some time and, ultimately, a change in scheduling.

But NBC still had confidence in *Seinfeld*. To prove its support, the network ordered 26 new shows, four more than usual. This good news resulted in even more panic on the set as the writers slipped behind in scripts as the season's tapings got underway. At one point Larry David had to write an entire episode over a weekend to be filmed the next week. He called it "The Contest" and it turned out to be the show's most famous — and infamous — episode to date.

"THE CONTEST"

That David could pass by the NBC censors a script about a contest of who can refrain the longest from masturbating was due to the last-minute rush. Airing on November 18, the episode broke one of the sacred taboos of television. Sponsors, not usually known for their willingness to take risks, pulled out when they heard about the subject matter. But other sponsors hurried to replace them, smelling the attention that the show would generate.

David based the episode on an actual contest that he had held with some friends. The inspiration for the contest occurs when George's mother catches him getting aroused with a copy of *Glamour*, falls down, and has to be taken to the hospital. There she asks George to get her something to eat, but he's so busy watching a nurse give a woman a sponge bath that he merely throws her some tic tacs. The word "masturbation" is never used, and the characters have a good deal of fun getting around saying it. Whoever can control the habit longest will be crowned "master of your domain." Even Elaine participates, a fact that some right-minded people considered particularly offensive. Not surprisingly, the irrepressible Kramer gives in first. After seeing a naked woman through Jerry's window, he disappears for a short while, only to come back, slap his money down, and declare, "I'm out." In the end, George and Jerry tie, although some viewers seemed uncertain; the actors would often be asked by fan who the winner was. The cast joked with a writer for *Rolling Stone* about a future episode where George, believing that the contest is still on, continues to abstain.

While NBC received some negative mail, the network received more letters that were positive. Most of the press wrote gleefully about the episode, but the magazine *America* condemned it as inappropriate family viewing and morally distasteful. (What else can one expect from a magazine called *America*?) Such attacks would be launched on the show occasionally by people who claimed to be protecting the nation from the immoral influence of Hollywood. One group, the American Family Association, took *Seinfeld* and several other shows to task in an advertisement in the *New York Times*.

This wasn't the only episode to raise a few eyebrows. Elaine Pope recalled for *Morningside* her introduction to writing for *Seinfeld*. "The first show we did when I got there was the show where George got a massage and his penis moves during the massage and he starts to think that he's gay. I turned to Larry [David] and said, 'You're doing a prime-time sitcom on homophobia and all these other issues and nobody's stopping you. Isn't that amazing?' And he just kind of looked at me and shrugged, like, 'Why shouldn't I?' He's just so strong with his vision and such a unique individual. He's been able to pull this off but it's really rare. I don't think there's any other show that does what *Seinfeld* does."

But Larry David doesn't just present a previously taboo subject and get away with it. Despite his never having created or written a sitcom before, and despite his avowals of not knowing anything about them, he has shown himself to be extraordinarily astute in knowing how far he can stretch the form. Larry Charles expressed his insight into this talent for the *Los Angeles Times*. "[Larry David] has the innate sense to take almost any provocative subject, find the right tone for it, and the right angle and make it palatable to an audience. I think that is part of his genius. He is totally fearless facing almost any subject matter, but he knows how far to go."

Charles was right; the great majority of people who watch *Seinfeld* are not offended by it. And those organizations and critics who are offended misunderstand the show. The intention of *Seinfeld* is not to shock — there are plenty of "infotainment" and cop shows to do that and, besides, Seinfeld rejected that kind of humor years ago. Instead, it treats as normal those things that television never even whispers but that everybody (well, almost everybody) knows is a part of life. In another episode from the 1992–93 season, a model who Jerry is dating thinks that she catches him picking his nose. (The incident was yet another based on an actual incident that happened to a writer on the show.) The closest the script even got to being crude was George's question to Jerry, "Was it a pick or a scratch?" But even that line was a comic take on an interesting social question: at what point does acceptable behavior cross the line and become publicly unacceptable? *Seinfeld* the show, like Seinfeld the stand-up comic, revels in exploring these minute social rules which we rarely question but which govern our behavior before others.

Most of the season's shows weren't quite so controversial, however. A very amusing episode, written by Peter Mehlman, begins with George meeting a pretty woman of Asian descent in the coffee shop who thinks he has a great sense of humor. When George hears that Cheryl's an immigration and naturalization lawyer, he asks, "What is that? Immigrants come over, you show them how to act natural?" Cheryl agrees to have dinner with him but when they meet Jerry and Elaine in the same restaurant (Isabella's, a real restaurant in Manhattan), George begs Jerry not to be funny for once. Jerry, insisting that his humor is completely under his control, pretends to be depressed and alienated. Struck by his seriousness, Cheryl asks, "Do you ever laugh?" Jerry intones, "Not really. Sometimes when I'm in the tub."

Unfortunately for George, Cheryl finds herself attracted to Jerry who she believes is "dark and disturbed." He is forced to admit that Jerry is putting on an act, causing her to dump him. A desperate George confesses that the whole thing was his idea. "That's how disturbed I am. . . . Nobody is sicker than me. He's pretending, I'm the genuine article." Sick or not, once again George is left without the girl.

A SHOW ABOUT NOTHING IN
A SHOW ABOUT NOTHING

While many television shows have at best a tenuous relationship to reality, Larry David actually looked to real life for material for *Seinfeld*. Wasn't, then, the natural next step to write about the making of a television show?

The official opening of the 1992–93 season, on September 16, was the premiere of an hour-long episode. Its conclusion would occur nine months later, with the one-hour season finale. After Jerry performs at a club, two NBC executives approach him to say that they are interested in him "doing something" for the network. Back at the coffee shop Jerry talks about the proposal with George, who comes up with the idea of a show about nothing. Although Jerry is sceptical, George, who wants to write it, persists. Jerry asks, "Since when are you a writer?" George answers, "What writer? We're talking about a sitcom." George's brilliant idea is that besides Seinfeld there should be a character based on himself, since everyone has always told George that he was a "character." Viewers of the show may not have known how closely the story mirrored the way that *Seinfeld* began.

When taping for the season began, the writers knew only

that they were going to set up this proposed television show in the first episode and show the taping of the pilot in the last. Otherwise they had little idea how the story would develop and even considered scrapping the idea several times. In one very funny episode, written by David and Seinfeld, Jerry and George are sitting on Jerry's couch writing the pilot together. They decide that the character based on Elaine should enter but then can't think of a single line for her. "What do women say?" Jerry asks. "I don't know what they think. That's why I'm in therapy," George sighs. So they decide to leave her out of the script — mimicking the fact that Elaine did not exist in the pilot of *Seinfeld* and acknowledging David and Seinfeld as writers who understand men far better than women. There's a wonderful moment when Elaine gets in a huff because another woman makes a fuss about her having bought a pair of shoes at the ritzy store Botticelli's. Jerry just stares at Elaine incredulously, confirmed in his belief that women are alien beings. When he discovers that Elaine is secretly thrilled that her shoes have become an object of desire, the look on his face shows that he now understands women even less. (One wonders whether the writer Elaine Pope had a hand in the scene and if she was brought onto the show specifically for the purpose of helping to write Elaine's part.)

George gives the pilot script to his therapist. But when she doesn't think it's funny, he shouts "This is what I'm paying you for?" Then tearfully he blames Jerry for taking out his best lines. "He's such a control freak!" The head of NBC, Russell Dalrimple (played by Bob Balaban), cancels the pilot after he catches George staring at his 15-year-old daughter's cleavage. But by the end of the show the pilot is back on. Seinfeld and David must have had great fun writing this one.

While the story of the making of *Jerry* (as the show-within-the-show was called) flitted in and out of episodes, it did not dominate the season. The lives of the four friends continued bumbling on, so that the *New York Times* could call the show "a brilliant riff on contemporary anxieties. . . ." As usual, dating was a major topic. George finds out that a former girlfriend named Susan is now seeing another woman. "You're just so hip," he sneers at her. The episode became evidence for a *New York* cover story that it had become chic to be lesbian. It was now a given that *Seinfeld* was a barometer of the latest social trends.

A long tradition of television shows is the Christmas episode. The set is decorated with a glittering tree and the characters play through some little dilemma about buying presents or convincing a member of the family that the season isn't all humbug. *Seinfeld* too had its Christmas episode, which aired on December 16 and was written by David from a story by David and Marc Jaffe. Elaine is convinced by Jerry to let Kramer take her photograph for her Christmas card, but after she sends it out to all her friends and relatives, Jerry notices something wrong. "Correct me if I'm wrong," he hesitates, looking at the photograph on the card, "but I think I see a nipple." Poor Elaine suffers a thousand deaths of embarrassment. At her office, the other employees start calling her "Nip." When George complains that he's the only one not to get a card from her, she grabs his head and shoves it into her bosom. "There's your Christmas card!" she rages.

Unfortunately, not all of the season's episodes were this funny. Near the end of the season one of the rare duds was aired. Seinfeld and friends visit a mall to buy a wedding gift for a friend named Drake but can't find a parking space. George finally parks his father's car in a handicapped spot, only to have it wrecked by an angry mob after a woman is forced to park elsewhere and is hurt when her wheelchair rushes down an incline. The scenario is the occasion for a lot of crude handicapped jokes that, besides being insensitive, aren't very funny. Later the *New York Times* television critic complained in print about the episode with complete justification.

It's quite possible that Larry David doesn't care about such criticisms. He seems to believe that the world is a cruel place and that making comedy out of dark situations (the smog strangler and the neo-Nazi plots are other examples) is a way of giving depth to comedy. If his characters crack jokes at the expense of a person in a wheelchair, well that is just a reflection of the way people really talk. To his credit, he has never tried to win over an audience by creating warm, ingratiating characters. Nor has he worried for one moment about political correctness when it means censoring his vision of life.

FAILURE IS LOUSY, SUCCESS IS WORSE

During the first half of the season, the ratings for *Seinfeld* steadily grew. People were talking about it and journalists were eagerly profiling its stars. But the show still hadn't reached the broad audience that a network can deliver. It was way down the list of most popular shows, hovering at about number 40. NBC believed that it could do much better and that its position on the schedule was the major factor holding it back. And so in February 1993, not long after the second half of the season began, NBC moved the show to Thursday at 9:30. What made the spot so desirable was that it came right after *Cheers*.

In any of the last number of years a lead-in from *Cheers* would have been a tremendous boost. Millions of *Cheers* fans were likely to catch at least the beginning of the show that followed and, if they liked what they saw, keep watching. But this season was even more special, given that *Cheers* was signing off the air due to the decision of Ted Danson that it was time for him to move on. The press had been feeding the public interest in the final season, building up to the two-hour finale in May.

Immediately, *Seinfeld* jumped with Superman speed to the fifth most popular show on television, with a whopping 57 percent more viewers. While the increase was due at first to *Cheers*, *Seinfeld* would only maintain that audience if people liked the show. It did even better than that; within a month it passed *Cheers* in the ratings.

Seinfeld didn't hide his pleasure. "It's just nice to have that stigma of being a cult hit removed," he told the *Los Angeles Times*. "I always knew we weren't a narrow demographic hit, because of comments I receive from the garbage man on the street or the security guy by the x-ray machine at the airport." But both he and David seemed a little dazzled. Seinfeld kept repeating that he was a stand-up comic first and foremost and didn't care much about television. Larry David tried to keep up his bleak fatalism, but it was hard to play the part of a permanent failure when you were the brains behind the hottest show on television. "The person I was then is the person I am now, only with more money," David insisted to *GQ*. He even expressed suspicion at the ratings leap after the move to Thursday. "Every day I pray that this show will be cancelled. I'm just a simple caveman," he insisted to *Entertainment Weekly*. "I don't understand why people are watching us now when they didn't watch us before. I don't have good feelings about anything."

As it became clear that the new audience was going to remain loyal, the excitement grew for *Seinfeld*'s own one-hour finale, "The Pilot," which was set to air just before the last episode of *Cheers*. In it NBC gives Jerry and George the green light to tape their pilot. So closely does the creation of the show *Jerry* mimic the making of *Seinfeld* that one critic, Robert Fulford of the Toronto *Globe and Mail*, called its confusion of reality and fiction "post-modernism for the masses." Never has television been so brazenly obsessed with itself.

Obsessed yes, but not necessarily in love. Larry David, who

wrote the episode, uses it to bite the hand that feeds him. The NBC executives are depicted as mere yes-men, positively evil, or — as in the case of the president, Russell Dalrimple — a juvenile romantic. Dalrimple is infatuated with Elaine who he barely knows, while Elaine is totally uninterested in him. She even tells him that she hates television, *especially* network television. "Come on, Russell," she says, "you're part of the problem."

George is naturally on the verge of a nervous breakdown. He tells his therapist that God will kill him first before letting him be successful. When the therapist points out that George doesn't believe in God, he answers, "I do for the bad things." The therapist notices a white discoloration on George's lip which George convinces himself is cancer. After seeing a doctor and taking some tests, he spends the rest of the episode in abject despair. While George's behavior is certainly in keeping with his character, this part of the story-line seems rather derivative of the film *Hannah and Her Sisters* in which Woody Allen plays a television writer who fears he has a brain tumor. On the other hand, both Larry David and Woody Allen are hypochondriacs, so maybe it's a coincidence.

Perhaps the highlight of the hour is the casting session, in which a series of actors try out for the roles based on George, Kramer, and Elaine. (In other words, actors playing actors who are based on real people.) The one who gets the part of Kramer, played by veteran character actor Larry Hankin, looks a lot like the real Kramer and acts like him too. The funniest subplot of what must be the most complicated episode to date begins when George suspects that the Kramer actor has stolen a box of raisins during the audition. Whether he has or not becomes more important to George than the making of the pilot.

The script for the *Jerry* pilot is taken from the lives of Jerry and company as seen on past episodes of *Seinfeld*, just as

Seinfeld is based on real events in the lives of its creators. During rehearsals, Jerry worries about his poor acting ability, mimicking Seinfeld's own limitations. But everything about the pilot of *Jerry* highlights how different *Seinfeld* is from most television. *Jerry* is given a sappy musical entry and credits, while the set is an enormous and bland apartment that could exist only on a sitcom. In short, it's what *Seinfeld* might be like if the network executives were allowed to interfere.

When the pilot is broadcast, we see characters from previous episodes watching and making comments — Calvin Klein, John F. Kennedy Junior, Bubble Boy, the virgin, the woman who thought Jerry was dark and disturbed, even Jerry's parents in Florida (his mother: "How could anybody not like him?"). Right after the airing, Jerry and George get a call from the evil female executive who has become head of NBC after Russell Dalrimple joins Greenpeace to prove his love for Elaine. The network is passing on their show.

THE END IS NOT THE END

The show *Jerry* seems to be dead and, unlike *Seinfeld*, will likely not get a second chance. But *Seinfeld* itself will go on. The writing has become stronger with each season, the actors more sure in their roles, with a deeper understanding of their characters and a finer sense of comic timing. Certainly its popularity has not yet reached its peak. The season finale was a ratings smash, with a 21.3 rating and a 34 share, which translates into 20 million viewers and number three for the week. With popularity came more critical acclaim. *Seinfeld* received an extraordinary 11 Emmy nominations for the season, more than any other sitcom. And *Seinfeld* won the Television Critics Award for Best Comedy.

A sign of the accolades that the show was almost sure to

*Jerry, Julia, and Jason at the 7th Annual American
Comedy Awards, February 28, 1993, in Los Angeles.*

receive on Emmy night occurred right after the season. ABC broadcast a new awards celebration, called the American Television Awards. Four hundred critics and journalists voted on the best television shows and *Seinfeld* swept the categories for situation comedy. It won for best show, beating out *Murphy Brown*, *Cheers*, *Roseanne*, and *The Larry Sanders Show*. Jason Alexander won for best supporting actor, taking the award away from his co-star Michael Richards. (In a funny bit during the presentations, Richards came on stage and tried to wrestle the award from Alexander.) Julia Louis-Dreyfus won for best supporting actress.

The best actor award went to none other than Jerry Seinfeld. Seinfeld accepted the award from a theater in Albany, New York, where he was performing his act. Dressed in a handsome suit, he held aloft the award as the audience cheered wildly. By not cancelling the engagement to appear personally, Seinfeld was sending a message to America. Despite the success of the show named after him, in his heart he was still a stand-up comic.

II

Seinfeld the Star

It is a sign of Jerry Seinfeld's rise to stardom that other celebrities now stop at his table to tell him how funny his show is.
He has been host of *Saturday Night Live* and a guest on Howard
Stern's popular and controversial radio show. "I love everything about being famous," he has written in *GQ*. "You hear
so many celebrities talk about the price of fame. As I see it,
there is no price. It's all free. You get special treatment every-
where. You can talk to people if you want, and if you don't
want to you don't have to. Why are celebrities always whining?
What's the problem?"

As if being a star wasn't enough, Seinfeld is now considered
an American sex symbol. Seinfeld thinks the idea highly amusing. "I've never had sex in my life," he joked to *People*. "Now
I symbolize it. I skipped the whole experience."

Oh really? Over the last year Seinfeld has been spotted with
more than his share of interesting women. In 1992, a *Washington Post* gossip columnist linked him romantically with Tawny
Kitaen, an actress who had been on *WKRP in Cincinnati* and
was known for her fluffy hair. The columnist asked breath-
lessly, "Could this be the same Jerry Seinfeld who was spotted
earlier this week having dinner at Manhattan's ultra-trendy

Café Tabac with *Sports Illustrated* swimsuit model Stacey Williams?"

If Seinfeld seemed nonplussed by the sudden attention of gossip columnists, he must have been less than pleased by the interest that the tabloid newspapers were now taking in him. The *National Enquirer*, a dubious source at the best of times, reported that he was dating an 18-year-old who attended a private Manhattan high school and was the daughter of a rich businessman. The paper ran a photograph of Seinfeld and the young woman taken at Madison Square Garden during a New York Knicks game. But this was the sort of attention lavished on a star, especially one with such an intriguing dating life.

Along with fame comes riches. Seinfeld soon took advantage of his high profile by signing on for his first major commercial endorsement, as a television spokesman for American Express. Ogilvy & Mather, the advertising firm, chose Seinfeld for a series of aggressive ads to encourage shoppers to use their American Express cards even when retailers try to discourage them. Seinfeld was given the unusual opportunity of writing them himself. "I love commercials," he confessed to *USA Today*, perhaps forgetting his anger at the critic Lawrence Christon for once writing that he had the sincerity of a TV pitchman. "Trying to do something well in such a short span of time is not really different than writing a joke." In one of the spots he delivers a lecture on drowning in debt to a goldfish. "He was really temperamental," Seinfeld joked about his co-star. "It was always, 'More food, more water, I want to lie on my back and float for a while.'"

The whole cast began to benefit from merchandising spin-offs. A line of greeting cards appeared, as well as such collectable kitsch such as coffee mugs. (One with a picture of Kramer has the slogan "I'M HUMAN IN MY WAY.") Seinfeld himself made an agreement to appear on a Kellogg's cereal box, a pleasing accomplishment for someone who is a cereal fanatic.

More opportunities arrived by the day. Seinfeld signed on with a literary agent at the William Morris Agency named Dan Strone, and soon publishers were making serious offers. The most attractive came from Rob Weisbach, a senior editor at Bantam Books, who met with Seinfeld's managers, Howard West and George Shapiro. Suddenly Seinfeld had a deal with Bantam and a seven-figure advance for a collection of his comic observations entitled *Sein Language*. The publisher made the announcement at Caroline's, a New York comedy club, where Seinfeld quipped to the 200 booksellers invited that he hadn't known that he was an author. "I do a lot of writing, but I never put the pages together," he said. "But if you leave them together on the pad, and number them, then you are an author." The famous portrait photographer Annie Leibowitz took his photograph for the cover, but the deal happened so quickly that the book still didn't have a title as Bantam began to publicize it.

Relative to other stars, Seinfeld remained restrained in his spending. In 1992 he did trade in his condominium for a large house in the Hollywood Hills, just outside of Los Angeles. Overlooking the city, the house has a magnificent pool. The truth was that Seinfeld felt a little uneasy about the move and wondered whether he would ever really feel at home in the new house. But as his mother told him (and he recounted for *Ladies Home Journal*), "Oh, it's always easy to get used to better." Indeed, the success of *Seinfeld* spurred a mini-boom in California real estate. Both Jason Alexander and Michael Richards also bought new houses.

A LIFE'S WORK

One of the dangers of celebrity for an artist is that it can isolate him in a privileged world, removing him from contact with the everyday life that provides him with material. Seinfeld seems aware of this danger; perhaps that's why his life has changed relatively little. One of his recent jokes has him pondering the mundane act of standing in a supermarket checkout line. "Very important, the rubber divider stick," he mused. "I don't want other people's items fraternizing with my items." Seinfeld needs to go to the supermarket, stand in line at the movies, drive his car in traffic. Otherwise, where will the jokes come from?

When Seinfeld says that his first love is stand-up comedy, he isn't just pretending. Between seasons of *Seinfeld* he goes on the road. In 1992 he sold out two performances at Carnegie Hall, where Michael Richards came onstage to set up the mike, tripping and fumbling about as the audience howled. On the vast stage of the Kennedy Center in Washington he gazed up at the tremendous ceiling and muttered, "If I have to work one more of these toilets. . . ."

About that performance, the *Washington Post* critic David Mills wrote that it contained "Nothing too deep." Yet he had the sense not to find that a fault: "good clean simple honest silly laughter is its own reward." Seinfeld's audiences are refreshed by his desire to simply be funny. His recent joke about attending a funeral, for example, has no worrying over mortality in it. Instead, Seinfeld calculates how long the funeral will take and whether he will get back in time to see the baseball game. "Depends on how nice the person was. But you've got to figure that even Lee Harvey Oswald's took 45 minutes."

Now when he tours, a driver picks Seinfeld up at the airport. But he refuses to drive in a limousine, which feel like "old whorehouses" to him. Also in 1992 he sold out two performances at the Auditorium in Worcester, Massachusetts, where audience members hung banners decorated with lines from the show. Before going on, Seinfeld told the security guard not to worry about his being mobbed. "This isn't AC/DC." But afterward Seinfeld was indeed surrounded at the stage door, only his groupies were elderly Jewish women. Knowing of his health-food regimen, some brought offerings such as granola bars, causing Seinfeld to wonder whether they thought he was a flood victim.

Seinfeld feels a little sheepish by the laughter his mere presence generates on the stage now that he's a television star. He wants to earn his laughs, not get them for free. "I want them to know that comedy is my life's work, that a lot of work has gone into this," he declared to GQ. "It isn't cobbled together after the show became a hit in order to make some extra money. It's not Suzanne Somers going on tour in Las Vegas after *Three's Company*."

Seinfeld receives a lot of movie offers these days, and his managers contemplate him moving into film the way Billy Crystal has done. The other actors on *Seinfeld* have been eager to take advantage of their new recognition. Jason Alexander and Julia Louis-Dreyfus were cast as husband and wife in the Rob Reiner film, *North*. Alexander and Michael Richards won roles in *The Coneheads*. Richards would also appear in *So I Married an Axe Murderer* with Mike Myers. But whenever Seinfeld has the time to do a movie, instead he spends it travelling across the country performing.

Seinfeld claims that he wouldn't care if NBC pulled the plug on *Seinfeld* right now, a not-very-likely possibility. Seinfeld would just go on doing what he loves. He has said that five years is the longest he wants to do the show and that he will then quit, no matter what its popularity. By his count, that would make 1993–94 the last season. "I just think five years is right, but you never know, I could change my mind," he teased fans in *USA Today*. "I just always believe in leaving before they want you off stage."

At the end of the 1992–93 season, *Seinfeld* had over 60 episodes in the can, just enough to go into rerun syndication.

After two showings of an episode (usually once during the season and once during the summer following), the rights revert back to Castle Rock, the production company. Now Castle Rock could begin to recoup its considerable investment in the show and start turning a profit. Seinfeld himself will make money every time an episode airs, ensuring that he'll be able to buy as many pairs of Nike sneakers as he wants for a long time to come.

However long *Seinfeld* lasts, it's unlikely that Seinfeld will be one of those comics who moves from one sitcom to the next. It's hard to imagine another show that could bring the best of Jerry Seinfeld out as this one has. And Seinfeld, thank goodness, is not the sort who secretly dreams of playing Hamlet or the lead role in *Man of La Mancha*. "My goal," Seinfeld told the *Washington Post*, "is to be like George Burns, but with more spinal flexibility." In other words, Seinfeld will do stand-up as long as he *can* stand up. And he is maintaining his Zen-influenced cool about the future. "I figure, whatever happens is exactly right."

WORKS CITED

Books

Blum, Richard, and Richard Lindheim. *Primetime: Network Television Programming*. Stoneham, MA: Focal, 1987.

Brooks, Tim, and Earle Marsh. *The Complete Directory to Prime Time Network TV Shows, 1946–Present*. 5th ed. New York: Ballantine, 1992.

Graham, Judith, ed. *1992 Current Biography Yearbook*. New York: Wilson, 1992.

Levenson, Richard, and William Link. *Off Camera*. New York: NAL, 1986.

Newspapers

Anzelowitz, Lois. "Seinfeld's Craziest Neighbor (and a Midlife Success)." *New York Times* 6 Dec. 1992: 11, 29.

Bianco, Robert. "Seinfeld's on Top, But He Still Trains Like an Upstart." *Chicago Tribune* 6 May 1992: C5.

Boedeker, Hal. "Seinfeld Faces Critics, Bertinelli." *Miami Herald* 15 Jan. 1992: 7D.

Cerone, Daniel. "'Seinfeld' Is Suddenly Something: Sitcom That's 'About Nothing' Finding More Fans in New Time Slot." *Los Angeles Times* 4 Mar. 1993: F1.

Christon, Lawrence. "Laughing on Empty." *Los Angeles Times* 17 Jan. 1989: 1+.

Colford, Paul D. "No Brains Needed for Seinfeld's Book." *Los Angeles Times* 13 May 1993: E8.

Coto, Juan Carlos. "'Seinfeld''s Stand-Up Sitcom Comedian Mixes Shtick with Scripted Scenes." *Miami Herald* 23 June 1991: 11.

Duffy, Mike. "Seinfeld Takes Success with a Grain of Angst." *Detroit Free Press* 12 Jan. 1992: 1G.

Elliot, Stuart. "Seinfeld's Jabs Give Amex a 1–2 Punch." *Globe and Mail* 3 Dec. 1992: B4.

Fulford, Robert. "I Hope This Clears Things Up." Editorial. *Globe and Mail* 26 May 1993: C1.

Graham, Jefferson. "Finding Snap, Crackle, Pop in Life's Quirks." *USA Today* 2 Dec. 1992: D1–D2.

Harmer, Ian. "Seinfeld Ready to Go from Stand-Up to Sitcom." *Chicago Tribune* 8 Apr. 1990: C22.

Johnson, Allan. "Jerry Seinfeld Ready to Join Ranks of Comics on TV." *Chicago Tribune* 20 Oct. 1989: 14.

King, Susan. "Seinfeld Enjoys Much Ado About 'Nothing.' " *Miami Herald* 15 Apr. 1993: 7F.

Mills, David. "Seinfeld's Amusing Patter." *Washington Post* 5 May 1992: B2.

Moore, Martha T. "AmEx Taps Seinfeld to Tweak Retailers." *USA Today* 24 Nov. 1992: B1.

" 'Northern Exposure' " Leads in Emmy Nominations." *New York Times* 23 July 1993: B8.

O'Connor, John J. " 'Seinfeld,' a Comic as a Comic." *New York Times* 7 June 1990: C22.

——. "Seinfeld's Quirky Road to Reality." *New York Times* 16 Sept. 1992: C20.

——. "Stand-Up Comedy Specials on HBO." *New York Times* 8 Sept. 1987: C18.

Pergament, Alan. "Success of His Comedy Series Surprises Unassuming Seinfeld." *Buffalo News* 16 Jan. 1991: B8.

——. "These Are Confusing Times for Jerry Seinfeld and His Fans." *Buffalo News* 15 July 1992: B12.

Richman, Alan. "You're a Comic. Make Me Laugh!" *Gentleman's Quarterly* May 1992: 136–41.

Rodack, Jeffrey, and Gary A. Schreiber. "Seinfeld, 39, Dating High-School Student." *National Enquirer* 15 June 1993: 24.

Rosenthal, Phil. "A Wry Look at Everyday Life." *San Francisco Chronicle* 5 Jan. 1992: 3.

Salem, Rob. "Seinfeld: Come On In and Join the Gang." *Toronto Star* 11 Apr. 1992: H1+.

Sandomir, Richard. "Here's One Loser People Really Look Up To." *New York Times* 24 May 1992: H21.

Seipp, Catherine. "Jerry Seinfeld, Straight Up." *USA Weekend* 14–16 Feb. 1992: 22.

Shales, Tom. "3 Minutes of Respect: Rodney Dangerfield's Comic Bit on HBO." *Washington Post* 6 Sept. 1986: D3.

Smith, Chris. "Turning Neuroses Into Nielsens: Angst-Ridden 'Seinfeld' a Surprise Hit for Stand-Up Comic." *San Francisco Chronicle* 1 Mar. 1992: 40.

Strauss, Duncan. "For Seinfeld, Money Is Good, But the Joke Is Everything." *Los Angeles Times* 1 Mar. 1988, Orange County ed., sec. 6: 10.

Thomas, Dana. "Names and Faces." *Washington Post* 18 Apr. 1992: C2.

Weinstein, Steve. "Tiny Issues, Big Laughs: 'Seinfeld' Earns Right to Weekly Berth to Toy with Life's Little Dilemmas." *Los Angeles Times* 4 Sept. 1991: F1.

Magazines

Bailey, Diane. "Julia Louis-Dreyfus Is Huggable But. . . ." *TV Guide* 3 Aug. 1991: 13.

Bellafante, Ginia. "Backing Green." *Time* 7 Dec. 1992: 85.

Calhoun, John. "Seinfeld: Getting That New York Look in L.A." *TCI* Aug.-Sept. 1992: 44–48.

Davis, Francis. "Recognition Humor." *The Atlantic* Dec. 1992: 135–38.

Esterly, Glenn. "Minutiae Man." *TV Guide* 23 May 1992: 18–24.

——. "Schmo, Schmuck or Schlemiel?" *TV Guide* 26 Sept. 1992: 8.

——. " 'Seinfeld''s Michael Richards." *TV Guide* 17 Apr. 1993: 4–8.

Gleick, Elizabeth. "Her, Sleep? Dream On!" *People* 23 Nov. 1992: 165–66.

Goodman, Marie. "Comedy Abounds." *People* 12 Feb. 1992: 87–88.

Hammer, Joshua. "Prime-Time Mensch." *Newsweek* 12 Oct. 1992: 88–89.

Kaplan, James. " 'Seinfeld': Manhattan 10024." *Mademoiselle* Nov. 1992: 80+.

Kasindorf, Jamie Russell. "Lesbian Chic: The Bold, Brave New World of Gay Women." *New York* 10 May 1993: 30–37.

Knutzen, Erik. "Seriously Bent." *Starweek* 12 June 1993: 4.

Lipton, Michael A. "Man Overboard!" *People* 8 Mar. 1993: 53–54.

Miller, Stuart. " 'Blossom' Blooms as 'Seinfeld' Sags." *Variety* 17 Aug. 1992: 22.

Milward, John. "Seinfeld Stands Up." *Boston Globe Magazine* 1 Dec. 1991: 25–31.

Mitchell, Emily. "On the Air." *Time* 21 May 1990: 73.

Neill, Michael, and Michael Alexander. "Success Was a Shore Thing Once Jerry Seinfeld Stuck to Being a Stand-Up Kind of Guy." *People* 5 Sept. 1988: 109–10

Rachlin, Jill. "What's the Deal with Jerry Seinfeld?" *Ladies' Home Journal* Sept. 1992: 66–69.

Randall, Stephen. "Jerry Seinfeld's Bland Ambition." *Playboy* Aug. 1990: 104+.

Schwartzbaum, Lisa. "Much Ado About Nothing." *Entertainment Weekly* 9 Apr. 1993: 14–21.

Seinfeld, Jerry. "Comedy Is Easy. Lunch Is Hard." *Gentleman's Quarterly* Nov. 1991: 248–55.

——— . "Confessions of an Unromantic Man." *Redbook* Feb. 1991: 62.

Stahel, Thomas H. "Of New Programs and Other Matters, Like . . . Well, You Know." *America* 20 Feb. 1993: 24–25.

——— . "Wednesdays in New York." *America* 22 Feb. 1992: 144–45.

Zehme, Bill. "Jerry & George & Kramer & Elaine: Exposing the Secrets of 'Seinfeld''s Success." *Rolling Stone* 8 July 1993: 40+.

Zoglin, Richard. "Comedian on the Make." *Time* 24 Aug. 1992: 63.

Reviews

"Seinfeld." *TV Guide* 19 Sept. 1992: 11–12.

"Spy Magazine Presents How to Be Famous." *Variety* 18 Apr. 1990: 41.

"The 43rd Annual Primetime Emmy Awards." *Variety* 2 Sept. 1991: 69.

"The Seinfeld Chronicles." *Variety* 2 Aug. 1989: 46.

"The Stakeout." *Variety* 30 May 1990: 55.

Television and Radio Programs

"The American Television Awards." ABC. WKBW, Buffalo. 24 May 1993.

Interview with Elaine Pope. CBC Radio. 740 AM, Toronto. *Morningside.* 18 June 1993.

"Michael Richards." NBC. WGRZ, Buffalo. *Dateline.* 29 July 1993.